PRAISE FOR

Unexpected Gifts

"In a world of stale religiosity, Chris Heuertz is a breath of fresh air. He's unafraid to ask risky questions and even propose provocative answers, but he does so with humility and grace. *Unexpected Gifts* challenges readers to consider that the supposed burdens of life-on-life community may be blessings in disguise. Read it and prepare to be changed."

—Jonathan Merritt, author of
A Faith of Our Own: Following Jesus the Culture Wars

"*Unexpected Gifts* is a rich and important book about the benefits and challenges of community that we desperately need. Chris Heuertz has lived out the message of these pages with great authenticity. His honesty draws you in, provokes, and heals, and shows you why community is always worth the struggle."

—Jud Wilhite, author of *Torn* and senior pastor
of Central Christian Church, Las Vegas

"Engaging and real, fascinating and gritty, Heuertz invites you to journey with him as he wrestles aloud with the challenges and surprises of life lived together. With insights collected from his experiences in slums, favelas, and neighborhoods around the world, he reveals the ugly myths that unhinge relationships. With a courageous honesty he speaks the unspoken questions that we all harbor, but are too scared to say. Heuertz gives hope, prophetic challenges, and an unexpected gift in this book."

—Nikki Toyama-Szeto, Urbana program director
and coeditor of *More Than Serving Tea*

"There are few people who can reframe the way we think or act and bring about a paradigm shift . . . Chris and Phileena are gifted with this. Their experiences are filtered through grace and the unconditional love of God, which Chris brilliantly articulates in this book. Fundamentally, it's a book about faithfulness to relationships. Anyone interested in leading an authentic Christian life will find wisdom reading it. Although Christian community-living is difficult, Chris challenges the common response of rejection within those communities. He suggests that the challenges can be converted to unexpected gifts. Chris is a brilliant and creative thinker of our time and uses parallel stories to contrast and expose the truth that leaves an indelible impression on your mind."

—Pranitha Timothy, director of Aftercare,
International Justice Mission, Chennai

"*Unexpected Gifts* is a prophetic book about the wisdom of community. For nearly two decades, Christopher Heuertz has led the community Word Made Flesh, whose goal is to serve and be with the most miserable and oppressed people of our world, hidden in war-torn lands, slums, and red-light districts of big cities. The community founded in the evangelical church has become ecumenical; members from different churches united in their desire to serve the poorest of the poor, are inspired by Jesus. I would hope that many from my own Roman Catholic Church may discover this new community clearly blessed by Jesus and the Holy Spirit."

—Jean Vanier, author and founder
of the Communities of l'Arche

"By sharing stories of tragedy and triumph, Chris illustrates an intricate picture of how communities come together in the beauty and the broken. His passion, commitment, and service toward others is evident through his vulnerable and transparent experiences in community. I feel immensely privileged to learn from these intimate stories of honest pains and true joys that stem from genuine relationships. You'll find yourself both challenged and encouraged by this gift that Chris shares with us."

—Nikole Lim, founder and executive director
of Freely in Hope

"Chris Heuertz's *Unexpected Gifts* is a clarion call to missional community as ancient as Jesus' first challenge for the disciples to 'follow me' . . . together. Heuertz's eyes have seen the glory, and his flesh has borne the scars of life together. As a result, his provocative and inspiring roadmap for community life offers insightful instruction for the next generation of saints while applying a healing salve for those who may have tried and failed before. Heuertz's book is an unexpected gift, indeed."

—Lisa Sharon Harper, Director of Mobilizing at Sojourners,
coauthor of *Left, Right and Christ: Evangelical Faith in Politics*, and
author of *Evangelical Does Not Equal Republican . . . or Democrat*

UNEXPECTED
GIFTS

Discovering the Way of Community

CHRISTOPHER L. HEUERTZ

HOWARD BOOKS
A DIVISION OF SIMON & SCHUSTER, INC.

NEW YORK   NASHVILLE   LONDON   TORONTO   SYDNEY   NEW DELHI

Howard Books
A Division of Simon & Schuster, Inc.
1230 Avenue of the Americas
New York, NY 10020

First Howard Books trade paperback edition January 2013

HOWARD and colophon are trademarks of Simon & Schuster, Inc.

For information about special discounts for bulk purchases, please contact Simon & Schuster Special Sales at 1-866-506-1949 or business@simonandschuster.com.

The Simon & Schuster Speakers Bureau can bring authors to your live event. For more information or to book an event contact the Simon & Schuster Speakers Bureau at 1-866-248-3049 or visit our website at www.simonspeakers.com.

Designed by Jaime Putorti

Manufactured in the United States of America

10 9 8 7 6 5 4 3 2 1

Library of Congress Cataloging-in-Publication Data

Heuertz, Christopher L.
    Unexpected gifts : discovering the way of community / Christopher L. Heuertz.
    p. cm.
    1. Communities—Religious aspects—Christianity. 2. Space—Religious aspects—Christianity. 3. Human geography. I. Title.
BV625.H48 2013
253—dc23   2012015798

ISBN: 978-1-4516-5226-0
ISBN: 978-1-4516-5465-3 (ebook)

Quotations at beginning of chapters from Thomas Keating are taken from *The Human Condition: Contemplation and Transformation,* Paulist Press, New York, NY/Mahwah, NJ, 1999.
Quotations from Richard Rohr are taken from *The Naked Now: Learning to See as the Mystics See,* The Crossroad Publishing Company, New York, 2009.
Quotations from Dietrich Bonhoeffer are taken from *Life Together: A Discussion of Christian Fellowship,* HarperSanFrancisco, 1954.
Quotations from Henri Nouwen are taken from (Ch. 6) *Clowning in Rome: Reflections on Solitude, Celibacy, Prayer, and Contemplation,* Doubleday/Image Books, New York, 1979; (Ch. 11) *Intimacy,* HarperSanFrancisco, 1969.
Quotation from Jean Vanier is taken from *From Brokenness to Community: The Wit Lectures Harvard Divinity School,* Paulist Press New York, NY/Mahwah, NJ, 1992.
Quotations from Joan Chittister are taken from *The Friendship of Women: The Hidden Tradition of the Bible,* BlueBridge, New York, NY, 2006.

Contents

viii

CONTENTS

Foreword

During the almost fifteen years that I pastored the New Jerusalem Community in Cincinnati, Ohio, there was a mantra I often used at the end of Sunday sermons. Eventually, the crowd joined in saying it with me, and each time we emphasized a different word in the sentence: "There is still so much we have to do together!" It ended the fourth time with the loud shout of the last word, "together!"

How true—and also untrue—this favorite mantra was. We did do so much together, so much that was very good, yet something much more was done *to* us. We were all changed and touched indelibly. But we also began to see that it was a school and a marvelous experiment in life, more than a community that could sustain itself long term at such radical intensity.

Our life together in those golden years of the 1970s, on the heels of the Jesus Movement and the Charismatic Movement, morphed into the hard work of sustaining our vision in the early 1980s—and not getting too bored or too hurt by one another while we sustained it. As always, the marriage was not like the honeymoon. The young people grew up, many weddings and baptisms were joyously celebrated, but those growing young adults rightly developed careers, educations, conflicts, and families that pulled them in other directions. They did not need me much anymore, and in time the radical, common-life households and shared paychecks all fell apart.

By the time I moved to New Mexico in 1986 to begin another "grand experiment," called the Center for Action and Contemplation, some of us actually spoke of community as "the C-word"! It was something we did not want to get embroiled in again—at least not any notion of intentional community, where meetings began to dominate, and membership requirements were always present and forever needed to be renegotiated. I began to have more sympathy for how the organized church had become so organized.

So now that we planned to keep on message, mission would be more important than "vehicle," and if there was to be any community it would be a by-product of shared mission. In many ways it was easier and less pretentious than sharing all things in common, but it also needed, and still does, all of the skills of relationship, emotional sobriety, forgiveness, love, and letting go that we needed to learn and live at New Jerusalem. And most new employees at a working center did not have those skills. Rather, they had to learn them on site and on salary.

In that early community, I had one of the young men paint "70 x 7" above the main entrance to remind us that forgiveness was the only way this would work and so this would be our new address. New mailmen were always confused, as were visitors. I often reminded the community that Jesus had given us this necessary guidance, presuming that even good people, people with the best of intentions, would still hurt and disappoint one another. "70 x 7" was not a mop-up exercise after an unfortunate mistake now and then, but an agenda for life.

I certainly needed such mercy myself on a daily basis, and the others needed it from me and from one another. Every expectation is a resentment waiting to happen, I always said, and we had very high expectations of one another. That was the name of the game, in fact!

Now, in New Mexico, we needed the same forgiveness skills because we also had very high expectations of one another and therefore probably equal resentments. I saw that this pro ceeded not from a community experiment but from the *human* experiment itself. Community or mission action centers are just life intensified—or human life squared. Somewhere, somehow you have to learn the skills—and the suffering—of doing life together. I am afraid it is a necessary suffering or you do not do much together—or even well—or for very long.

Thank God, and I mean that, we have folks like Word Made Flesh creating such training camps for Life Intensified. Chris's book, the one you now hold in your hands, is not just easy and enjoyable to read but filled with genuine insight, faith, and hard-won experience. It will open your head *and* your heart and teach them how to operate as one. What else would the task of any word made flesh be?

I am so honored to be asked to add my few words to the very good words already written herein—and to encourage this flesh that is loving God's world so well.

Fr. Richard Rohr, O.F.M.
Center for Action and Contemplation
Albuquerque, New Mexico

PREFACE

Setting the Table

Community—Why Bother?

If you want to go fast, go alone; if you want to go far, go
together.

—African proverb

One of the consistent metaphors for paradise in every major religion is that of a great banquet. When we gather at the sacramental table of community, we are, in essence, practicing eternity now. So let me set the table for our time together in this book.

This is not an easy book—not in terms of content nor in terms of the nature of the realities being shared. It hasn't been easy to write. It's confessional, more about making mistakes than celebrating successes. It's about the cost of community, not positive spin. In community, there will always be a series of losses, giving something up to gain something more. But in the giving up, we find better versions of ourselves. And that's not easy either.

So in the face of all that's hard with community, why bother?

It might be bad theology to suggest that the creation of humanity was predicated as much by God's love as by God's loneliness. Maybe somewhere in that thought there's an echo

In the face of all that's hard with community, why bother?

of an underexplored truth. After all, love, by its nature, is self-giving and needs a subject.

And if there is such a thing as divine loneliness, I imagine our need for relationships is one of those subtle indicators that we actually are made in the image of God. We need friendship. There is a deep longing in each of us for authentic and intimate human relationships. Could it be that we possess a sort of existential hard wiring for community, something that touches us in the most vulnerable parts of our identities and draws the divine out of us?

FAILING IN COMMUNITY

For as long as I can remember, I've found myself exploring this complicated part of myself, my yearning to know and be known. I've always been in a variety of communities. The most authentic ones are on a continual journey of failing miserably. In those circles of relationships we've let one another down and disappointed one another: Many of us haven't been the kind of friends we hoped we could be to one another. We haven't always fought fair. We've made plenty of mistakes. Sometimes we have given up on one another. But I believe tragic flaws bear unexpected gifts. I trust in the reasons to stay, even though I've experienced more than adequate excuses to leave most of the communities I've participated in.

I've grieved the loss of community members who could have stayed, who maybe should have stayed longer. I've lamented the ways in which I contributed to their premature departures and how I continued to fail them in their transitions.

Though some of the most complex community issues do not have clear solutions, the best of communities still work for resolutions that affirm the difficulties they experience. As I've stumbled in community, I've mostly stumbled forward.

FRAMING THE TENSIONS, STUMBLING INTO SOLUTIONS

The reflections throughout this little book illuminate the rocki est of my paths in community. These chapters illustrate what I've learned and am still learning. They are honest and vulnerable pieces of my story—a story that has been written in community and one that continues to be written through community.

This is a book about the unexpected gifts of staying in friendships, relationships, and communities. These pages testify to the discovery of unlikely gifts when we stay in community—especially when we stay after things get hard.

> **These pages testify to the discovery of unlikely gifts when we stay in community—especially when we stay after things get hard.**

The format is simple: I've named challenges many communities face and then suggest pathways toward resolution. But here's the dirty little secret: in community there really *are* no resolutions, only ambiguous and messy attempts to find our way back to one another. Attempts that, in our humanity, often create new tensions.

Ironically, as much as we yearn for deep friendships and meaningful communities, many of us seem to be unable to find our way into them. Even if we know we're made for community, finding one and staying there seems almost impossible.

Though we hate to admit it, if we stay long enough in any relationship or set of friendships we will experience failure, doubt, burnout, loneliness, transitions, a loss of self, betrayal, frustration, a sense of entitlement, grief, and weariness.

Yet it's these painful community experiences, these tensions we struggle to navigate, that hold surprising gifts. And so each chapter of this book introduces one of the tensions listed in the figure below, then offers ways to work toward the resolution.

TENSION	RESOLUTION
Failure	Support
Doubt	Acceptance
Insulation	Absence
Isolation	Inclusion
Transition	Stability
The Unknown Self	Identity
Incompatibility	Boundaries
Betrayal	Friendship
Ingratitude	Celebration
Grief	Contemplation
Restlessness	Faithfulness

Of course, the fear of experiencing many of these tensions in our deepest relationships is enough to keep us from giving ourselves to the intimate places of vulnerability in community, but when the risks are high the rewards are more satisfying than we could ever dream of. The very ways we fail one another are the clearest invitations into spaces that affirm our need for one another. If we can experience these challenges as reasons to stay rather than justifications to leave, unexpected and unlikely gifts await us, even in the most trying of relationships.

Stepping into community is far riskier than expected. It's far worse than you expect it to be. But in the end, it's far better than you could ever imagine.

We can do this. We can be better. We can do better. We can live better. We can find the courage to rest in ambiguity. Together.

> It's these painful community experiences, these tensions we struggle to navigate, that hold surprising gifts.

A TALE OF TWO LOOMS

On the south side of Omaha's Old Market district, just off the 10th Street bridge, sits an unassuming club called the House of Loom. An old, repurposed building, it's now a place of creativity and beauty, where all are welcome. With a tasteful Victorian aesthetic, the intimate space is framed by old brick walls, dark hardwood floors, vintage ceramic ceiling tiles, and a fireplace hidden in a little library at the back of the building. Local art hangs salon-style on the wall, like a shrine to our city's creatives. A discerning selection of liquor bottles lines the space behind a long wooden bar, said to be the oldest bar in the state. The dim pendant lighting is enhanced by glowing candlelight.

I first discovered the House of Loom's charm when my wife, Phileena, and I stopped by after work for a drink. We didn't leave until the bar closed at 2 a.m. Phileena is normally asleep by 10 or 11 o'clock at night, but the magic in this place kept us out. Old friends kept appearing and new friends kept emerging.

The eclectic mix of patrons was unlike anything I'd experienced—international folks, air force officers, hipsters, young professionals, and plenty of university students. Our dear friends Emily and Noelle, two women in a long-term relationship, spent most of the night standing at the bar with us. We chatted about life and faith. Noelle shared how she'd been kicked out of a Christian college—ironically named "Grace"—because she was in a same-sex relationship. We commiserated, and we listened.

As Phileena and I surveyed the club that night, we were struck by how accepting everyone seemed. Strangers bonded, friends laughed, and diversity was celebrated. People from all walks of life gathered in a shared space and felt free enough to bare their true selves. The House of Loom lives out its name—it's a place where the social fabric of our city is woven together.

On the drive home late that night, I couldn't help thinking about the depth of community I'd felt in that place. I witnessed more love in that bar than I see in some churches. Could it be that the House of Loom fosters community more than many Christian houses of worship?

Too many people think of church as an event rather than a community. They attend the church that they imagine can best meet their needs, but that expectation often falls flat. When they feel disappointed by the commodity they've bought into, they jump ship and look for a new place to worship.

Too many people think of church as an event rather than a community.

Yet I wondered how much the people we had rubbed shoulders with were committed to the community beyond the club's hours of operation. They were united around a common cause, perhaps, but how deep was their common commitment? Were patrons dedicated to staying involved if things got complicated? Were they devoted for the long haul? I didn't know, but based on the openness and acceptance there I suspected that surprising friendships awaited us. I found myself desiring to be more connected to this community.

The House of Loom had provoked a deep curiosity within me.

I've spent my life promoting the idea of community—how to create it, how to sustain it. About a half dozen of us started Word Made Flesh twenty years ago to serve Jesus among the most vulnerable of the world's poor. The language of community blanketed us, and we spoke it fluently.

Word got out, and soon people came to join us. But things changed. Those who joined us didn't know us, and many didn't stay long. Rather than friends who chose to work together, we became a group of coworkers trying to be friends. Though we were invested in a common cause, we maintained different ideas about what community should look like. Eventually, in some corners of our community, we began to lose our common commitment.

What we realized was that community isn't the romantic ideal so many believe it to be. It's difficult.

Community is made of relationships that demand hard work.
Community always comes loaded with expectations and demands.
Every community has its tragic flaws.
True community requires sacrifice.

Today many of the Word Made Flesh communities operate with a covenant process. If someone decides to join the cause, she or he can. All are welcome. But if they decide they want to commit, they enter into a covenant with the community, meaning, in essence, that we will bring the best and worst of ourselves together, that we'll submit our vocational decision-making processes, and that we'll remain open to the move of God in our lives as individuals as well as a community.

This small act expresses what we've learned—that community is not just a collective of people united around a cause. Rather, it's a group of people bound by a commitment to one another—and community becomes the loom that weaves them together. A loom that takes all our colors and pieces, fabrics and faults, and interweaves us to create something greater than ourselves. A loom much like the one I found in a small Romanian valley.

THE LOOM IN THE VALLEY

Galaţi, Romania, is the quintessential European industrial city. The Danube River slices through the urban steel factories that churn dark smoke into the air. Dull architecture of gray concrete matches the overcast winter skies. Galaţi's blue-collar citizens walk to and from work, keeping to themselves as they go.

Buried within the city is a small valley inhabited predominantly by Roma.[1] The residents here face poverty daily, and adolescents fill the streets. The children, most of whom can't afford to attend school, are headed to the Word Made Flesh community center, Centrul Comunitar "La Vale" (The Community Center in the Valley). There children participate in literacy classes, computer training, counseling, and art therapy. They receive hot meals before playing a pickup game of basketball, a favorite pastime of the young girls and boys who are reclaiming their plundered childhoods (many of them were sent to work when as young as six or seven years old).

A chapel sits quietly at the edge of the center. Though modest and unspectacular on the outside, the interior is a place of mystery and miracles. Our community members use the space as a contemplative retreat away from the chaos of the city. Each morning they begin the day with liturgy. From time to time, covenant ceremonies are held in the chapel. Nine icons adorn the walls, each representing one of our community's Lifestyle Celebrations, or marks of intentional spirituality (including, among others, commitment to mutual submission, personal brokenness, and an acceptance of suffering).

And then there's the loom.

Part of the morning liturgy includes praying for other international communities serving among those in need. In an effort to bring texture to the prayer time, community members built the loom to weave a prayer rug, which took nearly two years to complete. The rug now sits in the center of the chapel as a reminder of unity. One community member commented that the rug should be placed in the center as a "reminder of the centrality of Christ and those who are poor whom he weaves into his life in the center with him."

In their morning sessions, seated around the rug, they pray for mercy for our friends in poverty. Once a week, they take scraps of cloth they have collected from friends in our various international communities and weave those pieces of fabric into the rug. Each piece of fabric is a prayer, a reminder of friend-ship and community. The rug is always being created, never finished.

Today the loom is a symbol of hope, an image of unity. It's a metaphor of what is required to build and hold a collective of people together: useful only as long as it creates something more beautiful than its individual parts.

In community we join together lives that are bursting with promise and potential but that are also marked by grief and sor-row. We exist as individual strands of a larger narrative. When our lives are woven together with others', something new emerges—rich in texture, vibrant, and transcendent. The diversity and rich-ness that arise out of being bound up with others produces a holy space. It invites God to meet with us and among us.

Whenever our international communities gather, we engage in the practice of storytelling. We break up into groups of four to six people from different parts of the world and share the stories of our individual journeys. We refer to these small groups as "loom clusters." Each time we gather in this way, we're sur-prised to find unexpected connections between such different and unique individuals. People who have never met before uncover common experiences, mutual friendships, and similar reasons for choosing their vocations. We call these points of commonality "knots" because they tie the threads of our lives together. When we walk away from this practice of storytelling, we are always more confident that we've been woven together by grace.

My mind wanders back to the rug at the chapel in Romania, and a truth arrests me. Just as the threads of the rug are bound together, so the individual members of a community are joined.

To separate the threads of the rug, one would need to tear the rug apart and dismantle a composition of beauty.

So it is with community.

The contrast between Omaha's House of Loom and the loom in Romania is nuanced. In the former, we find good and true echoes of community: celebration, joy, acceptance, and diversity. The latter offers the same echoes but roots itself in shared space, lives, and spiritual practices.

> **When our lives are woven together with others', something new emerges—rich in texture, vibrant, and transcendent.**

Grabbing a drink with friends on the weekend nudges us toward our deeper longings for connection, but if we gather only to forget the week behind us, it's hollow. Likewise, serving and praying together without taking time to celebrate leave us longing. It's not a case of either/or. It's both. We need the echoes and the substance.

Together.

GRAVE STRUGGLES, GREAT GIFTS

Growing up in Omaha, a firstborn child and consummate over-achiever, I thought I'd be a fireman. Or a priest. Or a pet store owner.

I never imagined that I'd have to bury children I'd helped name. I could not have envisioned that among my dearest friends would be women who had been trafficked into the commercial sex trade or forced to work in sweatshops for companies like the Gap. I never dreamed that my inner circle of closest friends would include Muslims and Hindus. Though I celebrate my home and love my neighborhood, much of my life has moved far away from Omaha.

On Sunday afternoons during childhood, my parents would take us to our grandparents' house, where we would play street football with neighborhood children. None of us knew one another, but we recognized one another and that was enough. The familiarity and openness between strangers were inviting. My grandparents lived in their house for more than fifty years, and my grandfather had one job spanning the time from when he returned from World War II until his retirement. Life seemed simpler, and the predictability of that life made me feel safe.

Children saturated the subdivision where I grew up, reminiscent of the setting for the classic film *The Sandlot*. Following school each day, we'd climb a fence and tumble into the backyard of whoever was hosting the daily Wiffle ball, kickball, or soccer match. We'd pick teams, roll up the sleeves of our dingy jersey T-shirts, and play till just after dusk, when we could no longer see a tennis ball thrown over home plate. The diversity of the kids I grew up with seemed to diminish with time—as I aged, my schools, churches, and social circles grew more homogenized.

In high school I cultivated quite a few deep friendships, many that have lasted into my adulthood. So by the time I arrived at Asbury University in Kentucky, I missed my hometown friends. I recognized my longing for community, though I had little idea what the word actually meant. At that point in my life, community was defined by friendships.

It wasn't long before I made new friends. My six closest college friends and I did everything together, and we ended up calling ourselves "The Brotherhood." My roommate and I were two

Nebraska boys, but we found ourselves bound to a blue-collar football player from Ohio, a pensive and talented artist, two country boys from the swamps of Mississippi, and a philosophical missionary kid who had grown up in Taiwan. We discovered that what we had in common was more substantial than what made us different.

We traveled to the beach on spring break, as well as a few other times that weren't exactly recognized as "breaks" by the university. We prayed together, shared most meals together, and made memories around campfires. A couple of the guys wrote songs about our friendship that became anthems for our little community.

We shared our frustrations with one another, fought when we were angry. But we always drew back together because we had decided to stick with one another through the good times and the bad. One rainy night in my dorm room, we sat on the floor around a candle with safety pins and a jar of calligraphy India ink. We made a commitment in friendship and community to one another and marked it by cutting a tattoo into each of our ankles.

At the time, I never would have sat down and analyzed our friendships, but now I recognize that I was already awakening to the realities of true community. I realized the need for both joy and sorrow, for a common spirit and an obligation to stay. Those moments formed the foundation of the work I've done since graduating.

> What we have in common is more substantial than what makes us different.

Years later, I've found myself serving within a collective of contemplative activists called and committed to serving Christ among people in poverty. Our communities exist all over the world where we bear witness to hope—or at least the possibility of hope—that a good God exists in a world that has legitimate reasons to question God's goodness.

In some of the poorest megacities around the globe, we have set up drop-in centers and day centers for youth who live on the streets, in sewers, or in slums. We have established small businesses to offer alternatives to the commercial sex industry in some of the world's most notorious red-light areas. Our communities have opened children's homes, hospices, and a variety of advocacy-related programs that are locally owned and usually initiated at the grassroots level.

Weaving lives together in a community is hard, especially when you're planted in places like these. Our communities have wept over the premature deaths of friends, we've grieved over the atrocities we've witnessed. But we've done so together. Against the loom of community, the collective shares the pains of the individual.

THE UNTOUCHED ELEMENTS

Our community in Romania consists of a wide array of Christian faith traditions: Baptist, Pentecostal, and Orthodox. They live together like a laboratory experiment for Christ-centered, ecumenical community. A large black crucifix marks Christ as the center for all in the middle of the Romanian chapel. It is constructed of pieces of discarded scrap metal and other bits of industrial litter found scattered throughout the neighborhood. Below the cross sits an altar. During the community's liturgical ceremonies, the elements of Eucharist, the traditional Christian communion, are placed upon the altar. Yet they remain untouched—the bread never eaten, the wine never consumed. They abide as a symbol of lament, a sign of grief, a reminder of broken unity.

Since Orthodox and Protestant Christians have different doctrinal commitments regarding the Eucharist, the community is unable to share this meal together. The Orthodox priest doesn't allow our Orthodox community members to participate in liturgical services and prayer practices with Protestants. And the Protestants are prohibited from taking communion since none of the staff is ordained and therefore permitted to preside. At the communion table in the chapel in Galați, what should be the image of Christian unity has become a lament of brokenness.

But the loom calls us back together.

Though we exist as individuals, each imbued with our own unique identities and expressions of faith, the loom reminds us that we're bound together, committed to a common life. Our

> It's in facing and walking together in the struggles that we find the greatest gifts.

grief over our broken unity mingles with joy over our collective bond. From morning prayer times to evening ceremonies, the loom whispers a reminder that we are more significant together than we would be on our own.

This, then, is the "Why bother?" of community. This is what moves and motivates us to endure the inescapable struggles in community. Struggles that you will face, too, as your time in community grows.

But remember, it's in facing and walking together in the struggles that we find the greatest gifts. And although resolution may not come easily—or, sometimes, at all—it is worth it.

Failure

The Patches Make It Beautiful

The spiritual journey is not a career or a success story. It is a series of humiliations of the false self that become more and more profound.

—Thomas Keating

Lots of communities talk a good game about grace and acceptance, but when one of their celebrated members messes up, you find out how much they really understand grace. How a community handles failure—the failure of the group or the shortcomings of an individual member—demonstrates more than anything the strength of that community. And nothing can destroy a community faster than a spectacular failure handled poorly.

BRING ON THE PATCHES

My favorite part of every Sari Bari blanket is the patches.

Sari Bari is a small-business initiative that seeks to secure freedom and restoration in the red-light areas of Kolkata, India.

It offers dignity-ascribing employment opportunities to women exploited by the commercial sex industry.[1]

The name Sari Bari comes from two symbols. A sari, the traditional garment worn by Indian women, seen by some as oppressive, is an image of what can be reclaimed in a new way. In Bengali, the word *bari* means "house" or "home." Sari Bari is a safe home where women who have been exploited in the sex trade can find their humanity restored and experience a new life in the making.

Women are trained to make beautiful quilted blankets, scarves, and purses and then offered jobs in the Sari Bari community centers as a way out of prostitution. The products they sell are made from old, recycled saris, a symbol of restoration. Tossed-aside or thrown-away saris are recovered and cleaned. Something that appears used up, discarded, valueless is artfully transformed into something beautiful—even more, something valuable.

These products symbolize restoration. The process is a prophetic image of what the Sari Bari community is doing within the sex trade—allowing women who have been victimized and abused to recover their true identity.

> Something that appears used up, discarded, valueless is artfully transformed into something beautiful—even more, something valuable.

A common psychological coping mechanism of those who experience prolonged sexual abuse and trauma is creating false identities, or alter aliases, that they hide behind. Most of my friends who are forced to sell sex usually use a false name when they are working, names such as "Pinky" or others that clearly aren't the names they were given by their families. As a form of self-preservation, they externalize those aliases so that the abuse and exploitation they experience happen to their alter personalities and not to who they truly are.

In the early stages of Sari Bari's development, Sarah Lance, the project director, gathered all the women together to admire the beauty of their work. She held up some of the blankets and drew attention to each as an exquisite piece of art. Explaining that artists sign their name to their work, Sarah asked the women if they'd like to begin sewing signature tags on each of the blankets they made. The women agreed. When asked what name they'd like to use, in a surprising eruption of grace, nearly every woman chose her real name—the precious name given to her as a baby girl.[2]

Reclaiming their names is a significant component to the slow and patient work of healing, to the journey toward true identity.

A few years ago, Louie Giglio, Chris Tomlin, and others involved in the Passion Movement included Sari Bari in their "One Million Can" campaign. They identified eight organizations they thought were doing important justice-related work in the world, and while on tour, the Passion musicians invited one million college students to give at least one dollar each to make the world a better place. Chris Tomlin had a tour stop in Omaha, so we took him out for lunch.

Our community gave him a Sari Bari blanket as a thank-you gift for the advocacy work he had done on behalf of the women. He was kind enough to invite me to his show later that night. The energy was great—an electrifying light show with huge video screens and amazing music. Toward the end of the night, Chris dialed things down and set aside his guitar. He stood alone center stage, with a single spotlight shining on him. Behind a microphone, he gently held up his new Sari Bari blanket and began telling the sold-out arena the story of the Sari Bari women. He shared about the aliases the women took as means of coping with the horrific abuse they experienced every day. As he reflected on how the women each had chosen her given name to put on her work, he searched for the signature tag on his blanket. Upon discovering it, he said, "And this one, this blanket, was made by a woman named Mukti."

Surrounded by thousands of people in that packed auditorium, I suddenly felt alone.

I began to sob.

For much of her life, Mukti has been held captive in the small prison of her brothel room. Forced to have sex with as many as ten to fifteen men a day, she has been called awful, unspeakable things. But that night, somewhere in mid-America, her name was spoken of with honor and respect. Love was extended to her, and her story of grace and restoration was an invitation to worship.

A few weeks later I was back in Asia and recounted the story for the Sari Bari project director. She told me that in Hindi, *mukti* means "freedom."

Mukti, a woman named "freedom." We fight for the freedom of our friends enslaved in the sex trade, and Mukti's namesake inspires us to carry the struggle forward, especially when life gets difficult. Especially when the unexpected happens.

Freedom is beautiful, but, like all things, it has a dark side. Though hard to believe, some of the women we've worked with end up going back into prostitution. This is often the case with those who have been institutionalized, incarcerated, or systematically held in bondage for long periods of time. Their captivity ends up becoming an experience of security. In such situations, we all desperately need one another.

Each woman who lives into the gift of her freedom needs the others in her community. Every day the Sari Bari community comes together to create beauty. The blankets they stitch are vibrant, colorful works of art. I'm always drawn to the blankets that are saturated with oranges and reds, but regardless of the color of the blankets, the delicate little squares of sari material sewn on each quilt never fail to catch my eye.

Stitched onto every blanket, if you look hard enough, you'll discover tiny patches cut out of the same material the sari quilt is made from. Some of the little patches are intricately sewn so that the pattern of the quilt lines up perfectly with the pattern on the patch. Other times, the patches stand out, a bold statement of color that enhances the quilt's design.

> Freedom is beautiful, but, like all things, it has a dark side.

Generously added to some, sparingly on others, these little patches add a gorgeous layer of texture.

One day while with the women, sitting on the floor of one of the Sari Bari community centers, I was admiring their work and pointing out the patches, trying to communicate how beautiful I found them. Upendra, one of the English-speaking staff, overheard my fumbling attempt to get my ideas across and helped translate. He laughed out loud when he understood what I was trying to say.

He explained that each finished blanket is washed before being packaged. After they've been washed and dried, there's a quality-control check before they're shipped. It turns out that the patches aren't added to make the blankets more beautiful but to cover the flaws and tears on every quilt; they're an inevitable part of recycling and restoring each sari blanket.

Even more ironic, the women hate having to go back and repair their work. The patches are time-consuming and tedious. Yet it's the patches that make the quilts so beautiful and unique.

As is the case with us. In our own freedom, we still go about making mistakes, disappointing ourselves and others, living with guilt, shame, regret, or fear that the consequences of our worst moments will catch up to us. Many of us have a hard time accepting the flawed parts of ourselves when we're alone—a struggle that's even more difficult when we're in community.

SURPRISED BY FAILURE?

Every community is, at one time or another, plagued by failure. We all know that. So why are we surprised when people fail?

In my own community we routinely find ourselves wading through the murky waters of failure, navigating our way forward in grace while trying to retain high standards. The very things that make us great at what we do often have a shadow side. Many of us find that disturbing, yet if we are to receive the gifts of our vocations and benefit from the best of what our humanity has to offer, we must acknowledge our propensity to make great mistakes.

Why are we surprised when people fail?

In true community, it's vital to create a culture that embraces failure as part of our journey. That we keep on. Stumbling forward. Knowing we'll fail but failing toward grace. More than that, though, we need to know how to respond when failure comes. Too often in community, our response is less than grace-filled.

Usually it's a lot more grumpy and unaccepting than we'd hope.

If we can't give ourselves grace, we often won't let ourselves receive God's grace. When we don't love ourselves, we can't forgive ourselves. When we can't forgive ourselves, we don't let God forgive us.

Some of us feel that God can't or won't forgive us for some of our worst moments. I can't count the times I've felt as though I needed to plead and plead with God for forgiveness—even when I believe that God's already forgiven me. Painful parts of my past and present seem to haunt me, and I let myself think that God still looks on with unfavorable resentment. But it's not that God isn't forgiving us.

The problem is that we're unable to accept and forgive ourselves.

Here's the thing, though: if we're not failing once in a while—or for some of us, all the time—odds are good that we're not living a life that presses us into the possibilities and risks necessary to grow into the people we want to become. If we haven't failed, we won't know how to handle someone else's failure, making us harder to be trusted during some of the most fragile and vulnerable periods in people's lives.

To be in community, you must be authentically human.
Being authentically human means you will fail.

FAILING WITH FAILURE

Handling failure is sometimes harder than recovering from it.

In my experience, when folks are asked if people are generally good or bad, most Christians respond "bad" while most nonreligious people say "good." On a fundamental level, this speaks to our perspective on the nature of humanity. Our view of the inherent evil or benevolence of people is reflected in how we respond to our own and others' failures.

These assumptions also have a great deal of power over how we accept people in their failures. Peter Rollins writes about this in terms of our trajectory from belonging to belief to behavior.[3]

When a child is born into a family, she belongs; she is part and parcel of the home. When she is a vulnerable baby, there really is not much she can do to separate herself from the parents who conceived or adopted her. As she matures, she begins to adapt to the expectations of her family, learning to behave appropriately and live within the rules of her home. When she disobeys she may be punished, but she still belongs. It's not until she grows up that she comes into conflict with the beliefs of her parents, grappling with those values and coming to terms with her own.

However, even the most accepting communities, especially those who use *family* as a metaphor for what they desire to become, turn the belonging-behavior-belief continuum around.

To belong to many communities, especially Christian communities, requires a commitment to belief. Though disagreeing on subjective beliefs such as issues of faith should lead us to deeper levels of trust, disagreement too often introduces exclusion in many religious communities. However, if you do happen to believe the "right" things, you are expected to demonstrate the integrity of your beliefs through proper behavior. Once you've believed and proven you're able to adhere to behavioral expectations, you finally belong. So although community should be the place where we address our failures, communities often reject those who fail.

However, the most tragic stories of failure usually focus more on a community's mishandling of the failure than the failure itself.

Shortly after graduating from college, Caleb, a close friend I looked up to, made some awfully messy mistakes. Allegations of sexual misconduct surfaced from both men and women. There were also accusations of financial misappropriation. Questions even emerged about the authenticity of his faith. People I hadn't heard from in years were calling me, detailing shocking accounts and stories unfit to repeat. From all sorts of random places and people, his trail of shortcomings caught up to him. But the biggest failure wasn't Caleb's; it was that those who were hurt, disappointed, or angry didn't approach Caleb directly. Rather, they brought their concerns to me.

How did I respond? The more information I received, the worse and worse things seemed. I didn't know what to do. Incredibly disappointed myself, I penned one of the cruelest letters I've ever written in my life. I compiled the accusations, neatly structuring them in topical order, starting with the lesser sins and ramping up to a heartless crescendo of judgment toward his most humiliating failures. I signed my name and sent the letter

> **The most tragic stories of failure usually focus more on a community's mishandling of the failure than the failure itself.**

off. Not only that, but I cc'ed copies of the letter to a number of Caleb's closest friends (for the sake of accountability, of course).

At the time, I thought I was doing the right thing—the right thing for him and the right thing to appease my own value commitments. Now, though, I look back on that letter with profound regret. It was one of the worst things I could have done to him. I failed my friend in his failure, in his most vulnerable moment. I held my beliefs over Caleb's belonging and used his inability to live up to my standards as an excuse to exclude him. I demonstrated fidelity to a set of behavioral expectations rather than taking the opportunity to love. If I'm honest, I had been unable to extend grace to myself for my own failures, so I wasn't able to extend grace to him, either.

Fast-forward several years, and I suddenly found myself bumping around the bottom of my own life, my own failures. I lost my way. I lost myself. I gave up on the notions of my ideals. The standards I had held against others crashed down on my own head, and in the rubble of my life, I was broken.

Thankfully, friends rushed in to help me. People in my own community reached out, lifted me up. To my great surprise, grace was offered as I confessed my failures and did my best to find a way forward in them and through them.

In a loving response, most of my friends didn't mash me deeper into my failures, overidentifying who I am as a person with my actions. They talked me through the pain. They offered hope. They gave me the courage and hope that I would find my way back, that even if I failed again, those things wouldn't define me. They were patient, giving me time to grieve, confess, and mourn the consequences of my mistakes. When I was at my lowest, they climbed down with me and helped me up.

Years earlier I had thought my principled stand with Caleb was justifiable. But suffering the consequences of my own failures illuminated in deeply personal ways the real failure I had made years before, opting to cling to expectations or a love of my sense of moral conduct over the basic human call to love one another.

When I held my expectations over Caleb, I demonstrated a love of my set of beliefs and acceptable behaviors—making rules the subject and people the object, using rules as a standard for belonging.

But that's not the way of true community. In true community, failures give us the chance to choose people over principles.

Communities don't fail when they experience failure. The real and lasting failure comes when we use our broken and wounded members' mistakes to control them. When we do that, we perpetuate the strangling nature of failure, using someone's behavior to stoke the fires of shame, guilt, humiliation, fear, disappointment, or resentment.

> In true community, failures give us the chance to choose people over principles.

God doesn't use shame, guilt, humiliation, fear, disappointment, or resentment to motivate us or discipline us. Those are forms of emotional manipulation and abuse. They are punishment, not discipline.

Discipline is restorative and redemptive; *punishment* is dangerous and retributive. When we don't handle failure well, we push people away. We add to the shabby scaffolding of fear that keeps those closest to us from feeling the safety of confession.

I was wrapping up a breakout session at a large Christian music festival. The venue was a large circus tent; close to four hundred people had come to hear me speak about one of my books, *Friendship at the Margins*. After completing my talk, I had a little time at the end of the presentation for some Q&A. The first hand that shot up belonged to a young man, probably thirteen or fourteen years old. I anticipated what his question might be, but I—along with the rest of the crowd—was stunned when he made a brief and direct statement: "I'm addicted to pornography."

It wasn't a question per se but a statement of confession begging for help. The vibe in the tent shifted. My talk had been on mission among populations of desperately poor people, so his confession seemed disconnected from the flow of the breakout session. You could almost hear the gasps of people who were shocked, taken aback by the young man's statement. Side glances darted in his direction, some communicating disgust or disapproval.

> *Discipline* is restorative and redemptive; *punishment* is dangerous and retributive.

I looked the student in the eyes and thanked him for his honesty. And I meant it. I told him it had taken a lot of courage to share that with so many. I offered to find someone there for him to talk with, and after the session we did exactly that. But even now, several years later, my heart goes out to that kid and so many others like him. To those who feel so desperate, so afraid, that they're compelled to confess their most intimate struggles to a crowd of strangers.

Why does it feel easier to share our personal failures with strangers rather than our closest friends? We need support in our failures, and we need our communities to be safe places in which to find it.

SUPPORTIVE, NOT SURPRISED

We're not as bad as our worst moments, nor are we as good as our best. Those who are closest to us usually get this, so when we mess up they aren't surprised. Yes, during the darkest moments in my life, even when surrounded by lifelong friends and tried-and-true community, I have felt the loneliest. I have felt unsupported. My deep feelings of isolation perpetuate the fear that if I share my most vulnerable struggles, be they tender wounds or rough edges of my soul, the confessions will only lead to rejection.

And yet . . .

In community, I have been surprised by grace.

Grace in community brings us closer together, not in a way that creates unhealthy fusion but in one that validates the human struggle we all face.

> It takes a mature community to create the safe space where being honest is the expectation.

It takes a mature community to create the safe space where a culture of confession is celebrated, where being honest is the expectation. In those kinds of relationships we don't have to be afraid to share our deepest struggles or tragic flaws. And we learn that confession is the first step of truth telling in that painful dance of transparency.

Confession is hard, both making it and hearing it. It requires trust. It necessitates vulnerability. It invites the possibility of forgiveness. Communities that practice failure are communities that know how to forgive. However, forgiveness doesn't imply acquiescence. Truth telling means that we acknowledge the consequences of our mistakes. When consequences are part of our failures and accountability part of forgiveness, that takes us deeper into grace than we've ever been.

When we're afraid to confess, there's usually a corresponding fear that our secrets, our sins, and our failures won't be forgiven but rather held over our heads. But communities that forgive work toward wholeness and restoration. This is important not only for the individual who's fallen but for the strength of the whole group.

Restoration is one of those messy paths toward illumination. When we reduce restoration to formulas and checklists, it becomes another form of idealized failure. When we make restoration prescriptive, we simply reinforce the idea that the principle of restoration is more important than the person needing it. Instead, let restoration become a journey toward brokenness. For in brokenness, our woundedness is best addressed, our fears are calmed, our shame is lifted, and love is extended.

Of course, when relationships fall apart, moral boundaries are crossed, or laws are broken, there will be painful consequences. The fallout of these is often more than one can bear alone. That is where community can show up. That's when failure creates a place for an eruption of acceptance and love.

Failure, as an unexpected gift in community, creates opportunities to practice confession, forgiveness, and restoration. Sharing our pains and failures is a test of courage, as well as a test of the health of community. Grace reminds us that acceptance is support.

In our failures we need to feel safe. Shock or disappointment only pushes us deeper into isolation. And the practice of some communities, in which public confessions are demanded, sometimes lacks sensitivity and understanding. There's a huge difference between keeping something a secret and holding something private.

It's usually fair to be concerned if someone is keeping his or her failures a secret. Secrecy can lead to all sorts of additional problems—especially when we try to cover up our failures.

But as failures are exposed, an understanding of the need to keep some of these things private can be one of the most supportive responses community can offer. Privacy protects people in their vulnerability.

Failure has been the greatest gift in my spiritual journey. Failure has opened my eyes to new ways of seeing others and myself. Learning to love myself has surprised me with layers of acceptance and deeper understandings of grace than I ever imagined.

THE PATCHES MAKE IT BEAUTIFUL

Those little cloth patches on the Sari Bari blankets are actually sewn on to support each blanket and keep it from tearing even more. Rather than the whole thing being discarded, little patches are added to cover the holes. The patches are not randomly placed but intentionally woven into the blanket. The patches hold each quilt together.

It's the patches in our lives that make us beautiful.

It's kind of funny that something intended to hide flaws actually draws more attention to those flaws. Even funnier, the patches used to cover up the mistakes are what make the blankets so pretty.

It's the patches in our lives that make us beautiful.

After stumbling around in my own life, I now know the secret of the Sari Bari patches. I now see that people who haven't explored the gift of their failures aren't really safe yet; they're still trying to make sure the version of themselves they put forward is perfect, and they expect perfection from others. People who wear their patches with confidence are the most beautiful—people who've failed, messed up, and gotten things wrong are the most accepting and can be the most loving.

Wearing our patches, the little bits of healing and restoration that cover up our flaws and holes, brings extra strength and stability to the fabric of our lives and communities. It lets the world know that we're not perfect and we're okay with that—even more, that our imperfections make us who we are.

Beautiful.

2

Doubt

The Difference Between God and Santa

People of great faith often suffer bouts of great doubt at many
levels because they continue to grow at new levels.
—Richard Rohr

What does it look like to nurture communities that make space for doubt, for the honest questions we're afraid to ask? The questions we're not *supposed* to ask? How does community sustain us when we feel we can't go on alone?

In times of darkness or doubt, what is the role of community?

DISCOVERING DOUBT

I will never forget my first day in Mother Teresa's Home for the Dying, Nirmal Hriday, "The Place of the Pure Heart." I was still a college student, spending the summer before my senior year traveling around Asia looking for signs of hope, places of peace. It now seems ironic that I discovered those gifts in a place marked by death.

The Home for the Dying, the first project launched by Mother Teresa, is a hospice that opens its doors to women and men passing from this life into the next. During my first seven weeks there

I tended to nearly fifty dead bodies. On the fourth of July that year, a sixteen-year-old boy from a West Bengal village died in my arms. No fireworks brightened the sky, no hot dogs sizzled on the grill. That afternoon a young man's suffering and slow death exposed to me a different kind of independence.

It's hard to describe the level of devastation there. Some of the world's most graphic and intense human suffering is contained within the walls of that home. Though vibrant sunlight pours through the windows, the home is permeated by putrid smells of decaying flesh from those with leprosy. Its unassuming stillness is broken by a cacophony of hacking coughs from men and women dying a slow death from tuberculosis.

Somehow in that place I felt God's presence, yet I couldn't believe that God was really there. How could God let many die such horrific deaths while allowing others to live?

Directly across from a large, antiquated medicine cabinet at the front of the home was a special bed, the one reserved for the home's most desperate patient. Usually the man or woman lying there wouldn't live more than another day or two. Each morning when I arrived, it took everything in me to visit whoever was taking his or her turn on that mattress.

That bed seemed like the waiting place for death.

Above that bed, fastened to the wall, is a large black crucifix. Actually just half a crucifix—the legs and feet of Jesus are missing. Painted in thin letters beside the image of the suffering Christ is written, "I Thirst."

Could Christ's suffering, his thirst, some-

> Could Christ's suffering somehow be a comfort to those whose days were numbered?

how be a comfort to those whose days were numbered? I grew up believing that my faith provided clear answers to nearly everything. In the Home for the Dying, my answers didn't add up.

Through the years I've been guilty of tightening the frames of doctrine around the mysteries of God. I've done my best to hold to the beliefs passed down to me by my parents and churches. I grew up believing that everything in the Bible was true and that the stories were not myths but to be read literally.

As I've aged, however, I've become more captivated by the mysteries of God. I've been forced to grieve the security that my childhood faith provided. I've become enamored by questions rather than answers, allowing those uncertainties to press me deeper into faith.

In the Home for the Dying I was faced with legitimate questions. The unanswered prayers for life uttered by the men and women in that home forced me to explore the credibility of God's nearness to those in need. But I felt guilty about that. Doubt was just beginning to introduce itself to me, and I was unprepared to face it.

After living in Bangkok, Thailand, and working with people victimized by human trafficking who are trapped in the commercial sex industry, my friend and coworker Paul Rase wrote the following reflection called "Questions I've Never Asked."

How long can my baby live without milk?
Where will I sleep tonight? Can I find a place where I won't be raped again?
If I die tonight, will anyone remove my body from the street?

How long will this one set of clothes last?

Does being dirty on the outside make me dirty on the inside?

Why did my parents sell me?

Is there anything to eat in this trash can? What about the next one?

Do my parents remember me?

If I sniff enough glue or take enough drugs, will I forget how cold and hungry I am? Will I forget how lonely I am?

Why is the night so long? Does anyone know I'm in this brothel, chained to a bed? Does anyone care? Why don't they come for me?

Does the man I'm with have AIDS? What about the next one? Do I have AIDS? Is that how I will die? Will it hurt? Can I go home now, please?[1]

I've never had to ask those questions either, but I have a lot of friends who ask questions like them every day. Some of them are people of great faith, while others have been driven to understandable doubt. Their faith—and their doubt—have given me a lot to think about over the past twenty years.

> It's precisely when God seems the farthest from us that we most need faith.

It's precisely when God seems the farthest from us that we most need faith. Sure, most of us haven't had to ask the hardest kinds of questions, but many of us have questioned:

Where was God when I discovered the lump in my breast?

Where was God when I was falsely accused?

Where was God when we lost our child?

Where was God when I was being abused?
Where was God when I lost my job and then my home?

Often when such questions arise in our lives, God doesn't seem present. And when God doesn't seem present . . . we doubt.

What happens in our communities when doubt forces its way in? How do we get through these times together in community?

FAITH OF DOUBT + FAITH IN DOUBT

During the civil war in Sierra Leone, a few of us from my community visited Freetown. We hoped we could do something to help bring hope and healing to a nation torn apart by conflict.

At the time of our visit, the rebels controlled 60 percent of the country and a tense, unsettling buzz in the air constantly reminded us of the war. Refugees poured into the capital city. Merely driving through town was an assault on our senses.

We visited camps of disarmed child combatants. Boys as young as nine and ten years old had been taught to use automatic rifles. In many cases they were forced to turn their weapons on their own villages and homes. Children confessed unspeakable crimes—human-rights abuses and atrocities they had been forced to carry out. Those who had been victimized, who had become perpetrators, were now once again suffering the victimization of being further marginalized—living with the shame and horror of what they had been forced to do.

The refugee camps were equally hopeless. Entire households were made up of children. Little girls, barely adolescents themselves, now mothered the children of soldiers. We tried to be strong for Jennifer, who sobbed as she told us that, in exchange for her life, soldiers had tied her to a tree trunk and gang-raped her. She was only eight years old when it happened.

If I'm honest, most times I don't want to recall the stories we heard. When we came back to the States, we all needed time to process the secondary trauma we had been exposed to. Phileena, my wife, especially had a lot of trouble. She felt as if she'd lost her faith in Freetown.

Phileena has always been ahead of me when it comes to doubt. Only recently have I felt a sense of freedom to explore my own doubts. Over the course of our marriage, Phileena was in touch with her doubts. I was not. I chalked it up to our different temperaments. I figured that Phileena's feelings would lead her to places of great peace as well as places of great uncertainty, whereas grounding my thoughts in rationality would keep me confident in my intellectual defenses of faith.

For a while, that line of reasoning seemed to be an adequate coping mechanism. My certainty, or at least my perception of it, was a source of strength to Phileena in her dark times of doubt. What we did not expect, however, was that her questions would become a gift to me. That her doubts would remind me that what I *think* is true is still something I have to put *faith* in.

Christians believe some crazy stuff. Supercrazy stuff. Think about it: I'd be considered delusional if I came home one night and told Phileena that while I was at the market I'd seen someone rub mud in a blind man's eyes, restoring his sight. Or that a paralyzed person had suddenly stood up and walked. People would think I was bald-faced lying (or maybe even drunk) if I told them I had been at a wedding reception where someone had turned a bunch of pitchers of water into Argentine Malbec. Even my closest friends wouldn't believe me if I told them that someone who had recently died had actually come back to life—a full three days after decaying in a grave.

We really believe some outrageous things. To claim them as historical facts requires the humility to admit that what we believe is absurd and technically unlikely—yet we still opt, against all odds, to rest in a faith that allows us to believe the unbelievable.

When Phileena's honest wrestling with doubt and faith captures her imagination, I've learned to listen. It's true: horrible things happen to very good people, and the weight of Scripture would attest that God doesn't seem to want those things to happen. So when we see them, if we are honest with ourselves, we must find the intestinal fortitude to face them.

> One of the surprising gifts of faith, then, is that it's often not for yourself but for someone else.

Somehow Phileena's very real times of doubt lead both of us to places of lament—the grieving of the things that are fundamentally broken in the world—even as we simultaneously hope for more of God's justice, presence, and nearness.

Suggesting that doubt gives birth to lament is a luxury and not always Phileena's experience. But in our marriage, and subsequently in our community, when one of us has been down or experiencing doubt, we have found that the faith of those around us helps carry us.

One of the surprising gifts of faith, then, is that it's often not for yourself but for someone else.

"NOT THAT NICE OLD MAN, TOO!"

Though my faith is sometimes a reminder to Phileena that her doubt is legitimate, her doubt is a reminder to me that my faith is simply that: *faith*.

Our priest often reminds us that the opposite of faith isn't doubt but certainty. Some of today's Christian apologists would want us to believe differently, as if we could hold our religious beliefs not by faith but by reason. Faith isn't a formula; faith can't be reduced to trite theorems that logically add up and prove that what we hope is true or right.

This is a hard point to get across to people who argue against the possibility of doubting that in which they've put their faith. But it's not much different from believing in no uncertain terms that Santa Claus is real.

My parents were incredibly nurturing and gave me a great childhood, but by the time fourth grade rolled around, I think they were getting a little concerned about some of the arguments I was getting into. At school and in the neighborhood, some of my friends were beginning to learn the shocking truth about Santa. The news was spreading. But even when I was the only true believer left, I wouldn't budge. I fought for Santa's reputation of benevolent goodness. And why wouldn't I? Adults I trusted told me he was real. My social peer group had fortified the myth. And, of course, the routine evidence under our Christmas tree each year helped.

One day after school, Mom and Dad sat me down. They told me we needed to have a serious talk. My mind raced, trying to recall any mischievous fun I had participated in that day. I wasn't sure what exactly I had done wrong, so I waited to be reminded. When they started the conversation, I was caught completely off guard.

They began by telling me that the sandman and the tooth fairy were made up. Okay, I was cool with that. I had already lost all my baby teeth, and a dude who dropped pinches of dust in my eyes each night so I would rest peacefully was sort of scary (a nighttime breaking-and-entering character slipping into and out of children's rooms—weird).

But as they continued, I started to get worried. Next they explained that the Easter Bunny wasn't exactly real either. I tensed. My eyes opened a little wider as the implications began to dawn on me. I took a deep breath, and then my mom said, "There's something else we need to tell you . . ."

Before she could finish the sentence, with tears in my eyes, I said, "No! Not that nice old man, too!"

And with that I was devastated.

Here's the thing. I didn't *have faith* in Santa Claus. I *believed* in him. I *knew* he was real. Why would I have to have faith in something that was so obviously true?

I think a lot of Christians have a "Santa Claus" faith. Many of us, as children, read Bible stories as historical facts. In our impressionable minds, any questions about things such as the fantastic nature of Jonah living in the belly of a whale (I know, technically it was just a big fish, whatever) for three days were dismissed. We weren't allowed to question the Bible—it was the Word of God and so, of course, had to be true.

The kids who messed with me for believing in Santa all the way up to fourth grade were justified. Where was the proof? I mean, sure, there were always presents on Christmas

A lot of Christians have a "Santa Claus" faith.

morning, but none of us kids could ever testify to an eyewitness sighting. Come to think of it, Santa was arbitrary in showing favoritism: some of my friends scored big time, while others always seemed to be left wanting. Not cool. That should have been a tip.

My certainty in Santa Claus was nothing more than a fantastic abstraction, a fairy tale that I accepted as fact. I didn't need to put faith in Santa because as a child I trusted my parents not to lie to me. I believed in Santa.

I grew up putting that same kind of certainty into my belief in God, a nuanced substitution for faith. I had been convinced by authority figures that what they taught me was true. No questions asked. I trusted them.

As an adult I know better, and I know that for every Christian who believes in Bible stories, there are Muslims who believe many miraculous stories about their prophet Mohammed, as well as Hindus who believe in complex stories about Krishna or other incarnations of the divine described in their scriptures.

I've been in plenty of conversations with my Hindu and Muslim friends, and there's no real suitable apologetic that ultimately convinces anyone of anything she or he doesn't *want* to believe or was not socially conditioned to accept. What's most frustrating about those conversations is when someone, against all proof or logic, won't budge. The person who is absolutely certain that her or his version of the faith narrative is the only true story isn't a person of faith but someone who probably believed in Santa Claus (or one's religious holiday equivalent) up until the fourth grade: like me, this person is guilty of digging in with stubborn irrationalism.

Faith involves making an option for the absurd. Faith requires humility. Faith requires honest courage. Faith requires the maturity to confess that it is the optimistic cousin of hope—and hope is often unrealistic.

Therefore, doubt is necessary for faith. Being out of touch with our doubts is an indication that we're probably not in touch with the gift of faith.

THE DEVIL'S ADVOCATE ILLUMINATING FAITH

In the fall of 2007, the world got an inside look at the life of one of its most revered heroes. Brian Kolodiejchuk published a posthumous collection of Mother Teresa's writings to help bolster her canonization process. Ironically, rather than helping her cause, this collection provided a stark contrast to her public life of radiant faith. The media sank their teeth into the book and caricatured her journal entries in an effort to debunk the credibility of her faith.

Mother Teresa: Come Be My Light highlighted the doubts of one of our modern saints. It's an honest and confessional collection of letters and personal journal entries, full of very authentic struggles. In many of the letters to her confessors and priests, Mother Teresa wrote about her experiences of tremendous darkness. She shared shocking confessions of doubt—doubt in the very existence of the God to whom she had given her life.

According to the book, that profoundly troubling crisis of faith lasted throughout her entire adult life, more than fifty years of doubt.

It's actually the perfect sort of material for the *promotor fidei* (Latin for "promoter of the faith") or the *advocatus diaboli* ("devil's advocate"), who from 1587 to 1983 was actually appointed by the Vatican to stand against the *advocatus Dei* ("God's advocate") or *promotor iustitiae* ("promoter of justice"), who argues for the canonization for sainthood of a candidate.

I spent a lot of time with Mother Teresa, so with the release of Kolodiejchuk's book, I received several calls and emails full of questions about Mother's faith. Often my responses surprised the person who asked the question. After reading the book, rather than thinking less of Mother Teresa's faith, I actually found that my respect for and admiration of her increased.

What's amazing, given her crisis of faith, is that Mother Teresa remained committed to God and to her community. That is one of the most selfless acts of abandoned love: offering yourself to one whose love may not feel returned. Her confessions of doubt were also an indication of her honesty. Rather than lying about an unwavering faith, she had the courage to enter so-called forbidden places by asking difficult questions about God.

> Rather than thinking less of Mother Teresa's faith, my respect for and admiration of her increased.

Most of us can't even imagine the kind of graphic and intense human suffering Mother Teresa witnessed on a daily basis. In the three short years I lived in South India, we buried quite a few children who had died from malnutrition or AIDS. For me, their innocence and suffering were an assault on the possibility of God's goodness. But articulating my questions about God's nearness to those innocents in their deaths would not have been well received in a blog post or a holiday letter updating friends on my life. Who am I to question God's goodness, even in light of the death of an innocent child? Who is Mother Teresa to doubt God, even after more than fifty years of faithful service among some of the poorest people in the world?

When I read her journals, I felt relief. She doubted. And so can I. She experienced doubt, which makes me feel like mine is okay. Mother Teresa was honest about her doubt. Could I be otherwise?

What's remarkable about Mother's life—and too many journalists missed this when they reported on her journals—was not that she had doubts but that she *never stopped having faith.*

PROPHETIC COMMUNITIES OF HOPE

Through the centuries, the apostle Thomas has taken it on the chin. We've given him a new prefix to his name: "Doubting."

Shortly after the resurrection of the crucified Jesus, some of the disciples reported to Thomas that they had seen Christ. Thomas's response? "I'll never believe it without putting my finger in the nail marks and my hand into the spear wound" (John 20:25).

On the one hand, calling him Doubting Thomas seems pretty fair—after all, some of his closest friends testified to eyewitness accounts of the resurrected Christ. But on the other hand, Thomas's questions about Jesus's miraculous resurrection are critically important.

Rather than simply viewing them as his questioning the implausible, we can view his doubt as an invitation—for us to explore honesty in times of uncertainty, to affirm that faith transcends merely knowing, and to ensure that our questions are safe in community.

Community is an incubator in which faith and doubt can coexist. In tension and in safety, community is a place where we are free to ask tough questions. And when we don't have good answers or the doubts start to take us to dark places, community is there to remind us of God's faithfulness. Through one another, we experience eruptions of God's provision or comfort, miraculous answers to prayer, and the reminder of peace that God brings when we need it most.

Shortly after becoming the director of our community, I had breakfast with a mentor, Jayakumar Christian, the director of World Vision India and author of *God of the Empty-Handed: Poverty, Power and the Kingdom of God*. Ambitious but still anxious about the new responsibilities of leadership, I asked Jaya, "What is the single best piece of advice you could give to a community that lives and serves among those in poverty?"

Without having to think about it, Jaya replied, "Worship together."

I gave him a disappointed and puzzled look.

I had sort of hoped for something a bit more missiological or sociological, something about solving the great problem of poverty. I thought he might suggest the title of a book or a degree program that would prepare us for effective service. I even thought he might just encourage me to reread his brilliant book (which I have read and return to often).

However, in his usual way of simplifying complicated things, he explained that communities that live among those who are poor are exposed to painful realities that will inevitably cause their members to doubt the goodness of God. He said that worship is an affirmation of God's goodness *in the face of* suffering. Proclaiming God's love in places where love seems absent is a prophetic act of hope, and hope is all that some of our poorest friends have left. Jaya pointed out that worshipping together as a community allows us to carry one another. Some of us will have doubts while others' faith remains strong, and that polarity is necessary for a community of faith to remain grounded.

Almost twenty years later, I can say that that was some of the best advice I've ever been given. Over the years, I've seen a lot of people lose hope, give up on their visions of peace and wholeness, and walk away from God because they tried to face poverty and suffering on their own.

Somehow it's been the resiliency of our friends who are poor that has led us. I'm still surprised that the poorest people I know often have the richest faith. Though their faithful prayers seem to be absurd and go unanswered, in light of what they've experienced, they still remind us that when we lose hope we lose everything. They can't afford another loss, even the loss of hope, so faith is a necessity.

We all know that the doubts will come— they *should* come, if we're honest—but they don't have to *over*come us. Together we remind one another of God's presence, faithfulness, and nearness. We do this with courage and humility. We accept that doubt and questions are a natural part of faith; that they belong in our lives and our communities.

> **Worship is an affirmation of God's goodness *in the face of* suffering.**

Today I actually take comfort in doubt. It presses faith to demonstrate (not prove) itself. And there's no better place for faith to reveal itself than through the fragility of community— the space where doubts are safely explored and faith can be incubated.

3

Insulation

Forgetting the Fragrance

Let [those] who cannot be alone beware of community.... Let
[those] who [are] not in community beware of being alone.
—Dietrich Bonhoeffer

One of my favorite stories about Mother Teresa comes from my priest, Father Bert Thelen. He often recounts the experience of one of his fellow Jesuits who, while visiting Kolkata, saw Mother Teresa rushing across a street carrying a dying man.

The eager young Jesuit ran up to her and asked, "Mother, what can I do to help you?"

She abruptly replied, "Get out of my way!"

Sometimes the best gift we can give to our communities is simply to get out of their way.

One of the more difficult disciplines in forming community is making space for absence. This can be especially tough in the early stages of community formation because people hate to miss out on the life and rhythms of their community. But if the development of a community isn't marked by periods of with-

> Sometimes the
> best gift we
> can give to our
> communities is
> simply to get out
> of their way.

drawal, retreat, or other forms of creative absence, there can be a tendency for the community to close in on itself.

We came to understand this in the early days of our own community coming together. At the beginning we experienced much excitement about and anticipation of what we could become, what we could do. The possibilities seemed endless, and the scope of our reach seemed limited only by our lack of vision and ambition.

In the early days we did almost everything together. Most meals were shared at one another's tables. We traveled together on almost every trip. Most of us even moved into the same apartment buildings. Very little of our lives wasn't shared or held in common. That was important then and in many ways can still be important and appropriate for mature communities. But when that kind of pseudocloistering shapes the identity of a community, what inevitably happens is it fails to differentiate in healthy ways. This can lead to all sorts of codependency, emotional fusion, or any number of other forms of loss of individual identity within the community.

PRESENCE THROUGH ABSENCE

The writings of Henri Nouwen awaken us to the possibility of creative absence in community.

Nouwen taught at some of the most illustrious and prestigious universities in the world, including Notre Dame, Harvard, and Yale. He left academia to explore a vocation of service among people living in poverty. After spending time in South America and France, he eventually ended up in the L'Arche community outside Toronto, Canada.

Serving and living among adults with profound mental and physical disabilities was devastating to his ego. The core members of the community would never have been admitted into any of the universities he taught in, nor could many of them even read the books he had written. The core members of L'Arche didn't care if Nouwen was their priest or the janitor.

The loss of identity based on accomplishments, accolades, and acclaim forced Nouwen to redefine how he perceived himself. From the tremendous darkness he experienced during that time of desolation and rediscovery emerged some of the most provocative of all his writings and teachings.

Nouwen kept journals that he shared only with those closest to him. His friends found great comfort in the confessional writings tucked away in the pages of those intimate diaries and urged Nouwen to publish them. He resisted. The pages he had penned were private, so painfully vulnerable that he didn't want them read by anyone else. Reluctantly he did get to a place where he was able to offer them to the world. Sadly, the very week that his book *The Inner Voice of Love: A Journey Through Anguish to Freedom* was published, Nouwen died unexpectedly.

Almost annually I read that little book. The chapters are essentially pep talks. Two or three pages each, they are loaded with intense yet winsome little admonitions to sit in the darkness of nothingness and live the undramatic faithfully. In his chapter entitled "Claim Your Unique Presence in Your Community" he wrote, "Your way of being present to your community may require times of absence, prayer, writing, or solitude. These too are times for your community. They allow you to be deeply present to your people and speak words that come from God in you."[1]

What? Be present by being absent? When we finally find the community we've always longed for, the one that seems to meet all our needs, the community that answers all our heart's longings or validates the gifts we bring, we want to stay. We want to be present. We want to participate.

But absence doesn't take us away from our community. Rather, creative absence gives us back to our community in fresh ways. Nouwen went on to write, "Your community needs you, but maybe not as a constant presence. Your community might need you as a presence that offers courage and spiritual food for the journey, a presence that creates the safe ground in which others can grow and develop, a presence that belongs to the matrix of the community. But your community also needs your creative absence."[2]

Our communities won't always be able to offer us everything we need, nor will we be able to give back all that they need from us. This is tricky because sometimes we can't see it when we're submerged in community life. The insulation of shared rhythms and life sometimes convolutes our perception. That's often when we need to step back, to refocus.

> Creative absence gives us back to our community in fresh ways.

When I first came across that message from Nouwen, I thought I understood. Sometimes I use understanding as an excuse for inaction. Sure, I conceded, creative absence was important, crucial for the health of communities.

But actually pulling back? That felt like an impossibility.

BURNT OUT IN BUENOS AIRES

In spite of my own struggle to occasionally withdraw from community, the concept of creative absence stuck. We wove it into the language of our community. We even attempted to practice it. A few of our staff from Nepal and Peru went on "working sabbaticals," an oxymoron that caused more harm than good. They came back more worn out than when they had left. Seeing the consequences of their so-called sabbatical concerned us about the sustainability of our community's rhythms.

The early years of a new community can be quite exciting. At the beginning of forming a community, we led with our dreams. It was as if the only thing that could hold us back was ourselves. We threw ourselves into the work and had tremendous success. We experienced exuberance even in suffering. As we started new communities and opened new projects, the enthusiasm was contagious. Everything was a discovery.

A few years later we were nearly at the end of our ropes. We had gotten so caught up in caring for others that we had forgotten how to take care of ourselves. We were losing perspective. Our poor attempts at taking sabbaticals had backfired. The strains of living on the edge of slums and favelas were catching up to us. The constant loss of life around us started to take its toll. The natural transitions within our community had caused some of us to pull back in our relationships because saying good-bye to interns and an occasional staff member hurt. Could we keep going without them?

In a little guest bedroom of a modest Argentine home in Buenos Aires, we searched for answers. A full-sized bed filled the room, but sitting together with Adriana and Walter, two of our closest friends and dearest community members, we asked them about their own sabbatical. They were tired. They had spent six years in Peru founding work with youths who lived on the streets, many of whom were involved in prostitution. After spending a few months in Southern California to catch their breath, they had moved to Buenos Aires to replicate the work they had done in Lima.

It was cold that morning. We held our coffee cups tight, trying to warm our hands, and talked through options for real creative absence that wasn't simply good for our communities but good for us.

We discovered a real and felt need for space to reflect, time to rest, and periods of withdrawal for renewal. We discussed implementing communitywide routines that would make time for personal and silent retreats. That wouldn't be enough. We talked about protecting the Sabbath and ensuring that we took vacations. Still, that wouldn't offer the support some of us needed to allow our vocational commitments to thrive long term.

We imagined what the gift of receiving a sabbatical might look like. That cold, gray Argentine morning we started to draft a sabbatical policy for our community.

The idea was that after six consecutive years of community life and service, members would be offered up to nine months of sabbatical. We would implement a thoughtful application process that would include thorough contingency and succession planning so that other community members would handle the responsibilities of those taking the sabbatical.

Sabbatical is not an extended vacation; rather, it's a liminal space for renewal. Those who applied for sabbatical would need to identify opportunities that would offer rest as well as deep personal, vocational, and spiritual renewal.

It seemed so selfish at the time. The people who support our community's work make sacrifices to send in their gracious donations. How could we ask them to help fund our creative absence—a luxury that most of them would never have?

> **We had gotten so caught up in caring for others that we had forgotten how to take care of ourselves.**

Still, the policy was set into place. Though we recognized its importance, none of those who were eligible applied for a sabbatical. Phileena was ready, but I felt we couldn't do it. We were part of the support team. We were no longer living in a Majority World country, laboring among those in poverty—we were in Omaha.

One of our board members finally took me aside and explained that I needed to lead by example, that if our community members saw me take a sabbatical, they might feel freer themselves to take one.

> *I was hesitant.*
> *It was hard for me to stop.*
> *I was concerned that I'd lose grounding in the community.*
> *I feared that coming back from sabbatical, I might find I*
>   *was no longer needed.*

Despite all my concerns, though, after fourteen years in one community, Phileena and I finally went on sabbatical.

ON THE ROAD TO SANTIAGO

I tend toward the extreme. The middle is a hard place for me. Most of my life is lived as intensely as possible. I knew that taking time away from my community and my work would require a clean break, something so drastic that it would be difficult to pull me back in. No slow transitioning into sabbatical for me.

So Phileena and I turned our phones off. We turned over to our coworkers the passwords of our email accounts and social media apps. Thus completely unplugged, we jumped onto a plane and flew to Europe, laced up our boots, threw backpacks onto our shoulders, and found a starting point for the Camino de Santiago de Compostela on the back side of the Pyrenees in southern France.

The Camino de Santiago is the third sacred pilgrimage of Christianity, right behind pilgrimage to Jerusalem and Rome. In Santiago, Spain, rest the remains of St. James the apostle of Christ. A massive cathedral houses the relics. For 1,100 years pilgrims have prayerfully and contemplatively walked the road from all over Europe to the northwestern city of Santiago, finishing their journey at the Cathedral of Santiago de Compostela.

It took Phileena and me thirty-three days to walk more than eight hundred kilometers (more than five hundred miles) through the Basque country of northern Spain. Each day we'd stop at a monastery, convent, or pilgrim house looking for a bed. We walked through rain showers as well as the heat of the early summer. We walked through vineyards, farmland, mountainous terrain, and gorgeous little Spanish towns. Often we'd walk alone, but on most days we walked with other pilgrims—people from all over the world who became dear, dear friends.

The Camino is a self-guided pilgrimage. For the first week of our journey we didn't even have maps. We looked for tree trunks, large stones lying beside the trail, or street signs bearing simple painted yellow arrows pointing pilgrims to Santiago.

We got lost. We got caught up in violent thunderstorms. Some days seemed to drag on forever. More than once, after walking farther than we thought possible, we'd arrive in a town only to discover there were no free beds. We'd continue walking, sometimes twenty more kilometers than we'd planned, just to find somewhere to sleep.

I don't really like the outdoors. Honestly, I'd rather sleep on the streets of Cairo or Kolkata than go camping in the woods. And as an outdoor unenthusiast, I made the mistake of not breaking my boots in before beginning the journey. As the leather in my hiking boots softened and formed to my feet, the pain of every step reminded me that I should have prepared better.

I had thought that running across a crowded airport with my backpack on was sufficient preparation.

I hadn't trained either. I typically fly through Chicago's O'Hare International Airport thirty to forty times a year, and I had thought that running across a crowded airport with my backpack on was sufficient preparation.

I was wrong.

Our first day on the Camino was one of the most grueling of the pilgrimage. We woke up around 5 a.m. and started the journey. Walking down the back side of the Pyrenees wasn't the simple downhill stroll I'd expected. Rain began to pour down about two hours into the climb. Around the time we had planned on stopping for lunch, we crossed the tree line and the temperature dropped thirty degrees. The rain turned to hail. We had been warned about the mountain passes—a week earlier a pilgrim had died on that leg of the Camino. We later found out that two pilgrims had been hospitalized for hypothermia the day we started. Fearful that we'd get caught in the hailstorm and starting to suffer from the bone-chilling cold, we pressed on.

Some hours later, the hail blended with rain until ice was no longer falling on our heads. The mountain passes leveled out, and we found ourselves lost in a lush, dense forest. We had unknowingly crossed from France into Spain after missing a crucial turn and were now frantically searching for the trail.

Exhausted and anxious, all we had was each other. We kept slipping in the mud and falling into rushing streams of frigid water, and more than once we wanted to give up. Just before nightfall we emerged from the woods and stumbled onto a road. An elderly couple returning from the market passed, and we asked them for directions. They must have thought we were joking as they pointed to the large stone monastery of Roncesvalles just a couple hundred feet behind me. How had we missed it?

Those days on pilgrimage were some of the hardest in my life. Everything on the Camino became a totem, a symbol of my spiritual journey. Within days I had disconnected from the demands of my community. I was now consumed with finding a hot meal on the road and a bed at the end of each day.

My backpack became a metaphor of my soul. Throughout the pilgrimage I kept simplifying, leaving unnecessary and encumbering pieces of gear along the way. On three different occasions I packed up little boxes of things I thought too valuable to discard and mailed them home. Certainly I needed most of what I had packed, and as flawed humans we all have plenty of baggage, but some things in my pack literally slowed me down, and my body paid for it. As I emptied my pack along the journey, my soul was simultaneously cleaned out and emptied.

Early on the Camino we saw some Austrian pilgrims walking along the highway using ski poles. We got a pretty good laugh out of that. But after just a few days on the road our joints were giving up on us. Our ankles, knees, and hips felt the blow of every single step.

We had heard a rumor that a carpenter in one of the towns we'd soon be walking through was spending his retirement making canes for pilgrims. We found the village where he lived, which consisted of just a dozen or so homes. We asked around and discovered which house was his. As if he'd known we were coming, he had leaned two hazelwood staffs against the old farmhouse one perfectly sized for Phileena and the other for me.

With every step, our walking sticks reminded us of our weakness.

The only people I know who use walking sticks are older folks who need the help as their bodies have weakened. Yoda, the little green Jedi who's something like nine hundred years old, and Gandalf, the old, worn-out wizard from *Lord of the Rings*, also come to mind. Certainly those mythical figures possess power, but their staffs illuminate their weakness. Phileena and I lived with the sign of our limitations, needing the assistance of our sticks at every step. Making our way along the Camino, we emptied our souls, came to terms with our frailty, and rediscovered our need for community.

As flawed humans we all have plenty of baggage.

Markus, a German cardiologist; Simone, a nuclear physicist

from Paris; and Miriam, a pharmacist who only spoke Italian, became our travel companions. We must have walked two-thirds of the pilgrimage with our three new friends.

Walking together slowed the pace for some of us and increased it for others.

They say that less than 5 percent of pilgrims who start the Camino in France end up covering the whole thing by foot. Most pilgrims give in to injury or fatigue. But together we made it, walking the entire Camino.

Sure, being away from my community was hard, and the Camino was just the beginning. When we returned from Spain, we moved to North Carolina and were welcomed as Visiting Practitioner Fellows at the Center for Reconciliation at Duke's Divinity School. Again we were forced to make new friends, find new rhythms, and explore the possibilities of remaining vocationally faithful outside what felt safe and familiar.

The center rented us a little place to stay, the Rose Cottage. I remember our feelings as Phileena pulled into the driveway of the Rose for the first time. We were a little anxious and somewhat afraid. A new town. No friends. An empty home that we hoped would embrace us.

As we walked through the door of the Rose for the very first time, we found a big box waiting for us on the kitchen table. And a note. It was from a friend back in Omaha. Inside the box was a large and extremely beautiful bamboo bowl. The note read:

When you all arrive in your new home, you will have two things—a letter from me and a gift. It's a simple gift. A bamboo bowl. I'm excited because through this time away our friendship—not our work relationship—but our

go run errands–do body attack friendship will be deep-
ened. It isn't until we are empty—like this bowl—that we
can fully embrace solitude and welcome each other more
intimately in our lives. My hope and prayer is that you
can fill this bowl with love, memories, letters—and that it
brings us closer and close to God and each other. Keep on
walking Pilgrims.

During those first few awkward weeks at Duke when we were still trying to find friends, let alone our way around town, the bowl was a "safe" place for us. During our four months in North Carolina, the bowl was the centerpiece of our little home. It sat on our dining room table, and we slowly yet steadily began filling it with letters from friends, ticket stubs from games and concerts, wine corks, hotel key cards I collected from the rooms we stayed in, pictures of old and new friends, bar coasters, beer bottle labels, take-out menus, matchbooks, and other little memories from our sabbatical. When we missed our community and home, when we felt lonely and displaced, we sat at our table and pulled the notes and letters out of it and read them.

Months later, we returned to Omaha and were welcomed back by our community. To our surprise, the staffers had painted yellow arrows on large poster boards pointing us all the way from the freeway to our driveway.

Our town house had never felt more like home. But our first day back at the office was a little weird. Would they want us back? Would they need us back? Had the community moved on without us? Did the work we had previously contributed to still need to be done?

The members of our community also wondered what new ideas, big projects, or redirections we would impose on them from our time away. There were a couple awkward weeks while we reconnected, assuring them that we hadn't returned with more work or new projects for them, and they were glad to hand us back our roles and responsibilities.

As much as I had resisted taking a sabbatical, I finally understood how necessary it is. I returned with a renewed appreciation for my community. I had grown to respect and admire my people all the more while being away. It took stepping back to refocus the lens through which I saw them. Upon my return, their integrity, commitment, and selfless love for the most vulnerable of the world's poor invigorated my own vocational imagination.

Our being away was also important for the community. Our coworkers made a commitment shortly after we departed not to merely "hold down the fort" while we were gone but to nourish the continued growth of the movement. They led. They dreamed. They made major decisions. They encountered crises and worked through them. Facing challenges and embracing opportunities without us strengthened them as they grew.

The gift of creative absence also allowed for previously unimagined approaches to old problems, for fresh ways of doing things, and freedom to explore undiscovered layers of community members' gifts. We had to get out of the way.

Creative absence is one of those unexpected gifts that seems to benefit everyone involved.

Sometimes absence may be as simple as staying home on the weekend and watching the football game. Other times it may be as exotic as making pilgrimage across northern

Spain. But when our own hearts, minds, and souls are nurtured, we care for ourselves. When we tend to our own needs, we are able to bring better versions of ourselves back into community.

Creative absence is one of those unexpected gifts that seems to benefit everyone involved. We might feel guilty about taking time away, going on retreat, or taking a vacation or sabbatical, but as much as we long for those things, as luxurious as they may seem for us as individuals, they are also gifts to our community.

Creative absence suggests awakening to our own recognition that our community sometimes needs a break, sometimes needs space to reorganize itself, and sometimes needs the freedom to grow without the dominant voices, the typical expectations that sometimes stifle us.

Though I've gained clarity in recognizing my need for absence, it's still hard to take. My rhythms have become clearer over the years. I know I need the Sabbath for rest, retreats for reflection, vacations for recreation, and sabbaticals for renewal. All of which benefit my community.

FORGETTING THE FRAGRANCE

Alice Kim was the fashion accessories director and an editor of *InStyle* magazine. Her work took her to some of the most luxurious places in the world. While flipping through the pages of *The New York Times,* she came across an article about Omaha's Old Market, a bohemian downtown district with old redbrick streets packed full of cafés, bars, and art galleries. Something about the Old Market captivated her. She promptly quit her job, moved from Manhattan to Omaha, and opened a little shop called Trocadéro.

Trocadéro is located just up the street from my office. It's a lifestyle emporium, a boutique filled with handbags, shoes, designer Japanese toys, and hand-pressed stationery. Tucked away on the shelves are handwritten notes from some of the world's leading designers, "Good luck in Omaha, Alice!" and other good wishes.

When friends come to Omaha for a visit, I take them by the shop to introduce them to Alice. Recently Phileena and I were hosting a guest from Atlanta, and I wanted him to meet Alice.

As soon as we walked through the door we were hit in the face by a thick fragrance of exquisite perfume that almost knocked us over. Literally thousands of dollars of designer perfume bottles fill the little shop with their heavenly scents.

I asked the young woman working that afternoon if Alice was around. Sadly, we had just missed her. I inhaled again. "This place smells dreamy. It must be amazing to work in here all day."

She replied, "I don't even notice it anymore."

How tragic.

What a waste.

She misses out on the enjoyment of the fragrance because she's too familiar with it. She has to withdraw from the fragrance to remember that it is there. She has to leave the store and clear her head so that when she returns she can experience the beauty of being there.

So, too, do we in community.

Isolation

Re-Membering the Baby

The exclusion of the weak and insignificant, the seemingly
useless people, from a Christian community may actually
mean the exclusion of Christ.
　　　　　　　—Dietrich Bonhoeffer

My first trip to Freetown, Sierra Leone, happened toward the
end of the county's brutal civil war and took me to a camp
for the war wounded. It felt more like a massive slum built
around open sewers. The camp was packed with thousands of
survivors, but they were only a fraction of the wounded. It's
estimated that as many as 250,000 of Sierra Leone's 7 million
inhabitants had arms or legs amputated by the warring fac-
tions.

Burned into my memory are images of the brutalized. Nearly
everyone we met in that camp seemed eager to tell us their
trauma stories, recounting the split seconds that would forever
change their lives.

A young man narrated how he had been given a shocking
choice: long sleeves or short sleeves—meaning it was up to him
how much arm he'd like to keep.

One man removed his wedding ring, slipping it into a front shirt pocket before his hands were chopped off. Another remembered the last embrace of a loved one—before the arms that had held him were gone.

My head was spinning. I noticed a young woman, probably in her early twenties, watching us, leaning in the shadows against her little shack. She was one of the few adults who still had both arms and both legs. I approached her with my friend Jon, a photojournalist who had accompanied us. Unlike everyone else, Sophia didn't want to talk. However, her neighbors volunteered her story.

Sophia's village had been attacked, her home leveled by fire. She had been raped and her husband forced to watch. And then he had been killed.

While Sophia lay humiliated, sobbing in the dirt, her eyes drifted to the place where her now-fatherless daughter lay. Little Grace was only three months old. Following Sophia's glance, the rebels promptly grabbed the baby. One of the most horrific stories I've ever heard followed: the rebels took a machete and chopped Grace's left arm off just above the elbow.

Speechless, I couldn't believe what I was hearing. Until I saw her. Wearing a yellow dress, sitting on the ground just ten feet from where Jon and I stood, a three-year-old girl stared back at us. Grace was struggling—to no avail—to open a peanut.

That moment with Grace and her mother is seared into my memory for what it taught me about human suffering—and for what it revealed to me about the struggle we face in community.

Consider the words of St. Paul, the author of much of the New Testament: "The body is one, even though it has many parts; all the parts—many though they are—comprise a single body. . . . God put all the different parts into one body on purpose. If all the parts were alike, where would the body be? . . . God has so constructed the body as to give greater honor to the lowly members, that there may be no dissension in the body, but that all the members may be concerned for one another. If one member suffers, all the members suffer with it; if one member is honored, all the members share its joy. You, then, are the body of Christ, and each of you is a member of it." (1 Corinthians 12:12–28)

> "You, then, are the body of Christ, and each of you is a member of it." (1 Corinthians 12:28)

Too often, like little Grace, our communities are missing something vital. We're fractured and divided. But unlike Grace's, the losses we experience aren't something visited upon us. The sad truth is that we are the ones cutting off needed parts of the body of community, leaving us unable to participate in many of the activities community was designed for.

THE BODY MADE WHOLE

How diverse are our friendships? How complete are our communities?

Here's a simple test to try: Take out your cell phone and review the last ten calls you made or texts you sent. Who's on that list? What names come up? How many of our recently contacted friends are people of a different race, ethnicity, or nationality? Do any names of folks outside our age bracket show up? For Christians, how many people on our call lists are Hindu, Muslim, Jewish, or even nonreligious? What about their sexual orientation? What does our circle of friends communicate to people whose sexual preferences are different from ours? How inclusive or isolated is our call history?

Not that one's cell phone usage is the singular measure of the diversity in relationships, but for many people, the folks whose names appear in the call history staring back at us from our phones look a lot like we do. Many of us have a homogenized circle of friends who live like us, look like us, and probably even worship like us. Our call history is often a mirror of who we are. And, as a consequence, of who our community is.

THE DANGER OF FALSE CENTERS

I interact with a lot of groups that are compelled to draw deep, exclusionary lines to protect themselves. Even the community I'm a part of has been criticized for being exclusive.

Over the years, one of my dear Muslim friends, Mansoor, has asked if he could join our community. Mansoor has a huge heart, filled with compassion for people in poverty. In fact, he is one of the most compassionate men I know. But as a Christian community, our love for Christ compels us and unites us in service. I don't mean to imply that Christians have cornered the market on helping people who are poor. But our community doesn't simply help those in need; we serve Christ among those who are poor. This core motivation is what holds us together in community, not for the sake of artificial compounds or communes but toward the possibility of creating an inclusionary space for those who need to be accepted.

The nuances here are tricky to navigate because, as a community, we do not discriminate in regard to whom we serve or offer assistance. Many of the women we've helped out of the commercial sex industry are Muslim or Hindu, and the jobs we've created with and for them will not be taken away from them if they don't convert to Christianity.

However, did you notice earlier in this chapter how I described Mansoor? I introduced Mansoor by his religion, which is different from mine. These kinds of introductory qualifiers point to the false centers we subconsciously build around ourselves. These false centers tend to draw soft lines of exclusion by fortifying who we are as juxtaposed with what makes others different.

> **These kinds of introductory qualifiers point to our subconscious false centers.**

Brent Graeve is one of my dearest friends. Having grown up in the same town with him, traveled through Asia with him, and even lived in the same flat in India, I have some epic stories about Brent. But not once do I remember ever starting a story about him with any of these sorts of qualifiers: "My white heterosexual Protestant American friend Brent . . ."

I guess I don't use those qualifiers because the false center I project is of a white heterosexual Protestant American male. That's why people who are like me are frequently guilty of starting sentences such as "my gay friend Michael" or "my black friend Sharif" or "my Jewish friend Beth" or "my Mexican friend Cesia," or whatever makes us different.

You see, my false center, or what I claim as normative (white, Christian, heterosexual, and American) qualifies everything and everyone else around me by how they are different from me. I am my own false center.

I use my false center to label everyone around me. The more

differentiated someone is from me, especially based on her or his nationality, religion, or sexuality, the more I use descriptive terms to highlight our differences.

Since recognizing this, I've tried to listen to myself and bring balance to how I speak of others. Perhaps it's an overcorrection, but I've caught myself tucking little qualifiers into normal conversation, such as "my white friend Carol" or "my heterosexual friend Tim," only to have people look at me surprised and ask, "Why did you say that?" Ironically, they are often the same people who don't call me out when I say things like "my Muslim friend" or "my Korean-American friend."

> I am my own
> false center.

Sure, it's possible, and more likely probable in most cases, that our false centers are simply an identification with the groups to which we belong. It's usually unintentionally fortified and almost always perpetuated without negative or harmful motivations. But when we don't recognize the false center we've created in ourselves, we perpetuate exclusive environments that overidentify people by their differences in relation to us.

Which is why it's important for those who want to live in community to dismantle those false centers, to work toward an inclusionary posture grounded in love.

CONFESSING THE POVERTY OF OUR FRIENDSHIPS

Recognizing the subtlety of our false centers will help many of us confess the poverty of our friendships. When we desire our cell phone call history to look a little more diverse or a bit more inclusive than it currently is, we've arrived at a point that is, first, accepting of ourselves and, second, can better accept the so-called other.

I sit on several boards of directors for various nonprofit organizations. Typically, they consist of middle-aged affluent white men. A few of the boards have had an awakening awareness of their homogenization, which has led to sincere efforts to cre ate more authentically inclusive membership. But this enlightenment, though marked by good intentions, is sometimes painful to observe.

At one meeting, a board I served on was talking about recruiting some "multicultural" (read: nonwhite) members. The intention was widely validated and encouraged by everyone around the table, but when the group started brainstorming a list of potential candidates, it quickly became obvious that most of the names suggested were "personalities" or celebrity-esque public figures whom no one at the table actually knew. It was quite an impressive list, had anyone at the table actually known anyone who was being suggested. An honest review of the list was indicative of the poverty of friendships around the table, illustrating the lack of a broad and deep circle of friendships made up of people different from those generating the list.

Until we confess the poverty of our friendships, many of our attempts to foster inclusion run the risk of becoming awkward and inappropriate efforts of tokenism. It doesn't feel good to be the "token" anything in any community. It diminishes everyone's humanity to be misled by communities that appear to be inclusive but are actually using minority members for cosmetic purposes.

This happens a lot in materials used to recruit members for various communities. I went to a college with very few black students, most of whom were from Africa, not African Americans. But if you looked at the campus website or any of the college's promotional materials, you'd almost always see an ethnically diverse group of smiling students—strikingly disproportionate to the actual demographics of the student population.

Pick up a popular Christian magazine that has advertisements for North American seminaries or universities, and you'll probably notice that many of the students pictured are nonwhite. However, if you visit those same campuses, it's more than likely you'll notice a white-majority student population that is more homogenized than the projected or desired community makeup. Sadly, tokenism is rampant even in Christian circles, and the poverty of relationships evident in many of these circles can't be overcome by picturing the ideal when it's not reflective of the reality.

Over the years I've had to face my own fumbling around in these areas. I've made lots of mistakes, hoping that I was stumbling forward in open-mindedness, and I've attempted to form a more accepting and inclusive community at the expense of human dignity. I've had to learn the mutual burden of responsibility, but I've also learned that we might have a greater blind spot if our false center is normative or privileged.

Making choices based on love is always the safest way to nurture friendships and community.

What I've learned is that making choices based on love—love of people—is always the safest way to nurture friendships and community.

In community, we need to ask ourselves the "why" questions:

Why are our communities so homogenized?
Why does my circle of friends lack diversity?

These questions lead to harder questions, such as "Am I fortifying the false centers of my preferences, standards of morality, or ethnic identity?" And "What are the implications of that, both for me personally and for my community?"

FOCUS ISN'T EXCLUSION

Inclusion is one of those concepts that sometimes causes a reaction in folks because of the assumptions associated with it. Religious people often assume that inclusion in their communities will lead to an acquiescence of values—that including the so-called other (folks not living in accordance with the convictions of a particular community, people of different faith, sexual orientation, or a variety of other nonnormative qualifiers based on the core set of a community's beliefs) will force concessions or compromise convictions.

Sadly, this illuminates the often unconscious choice for values over the choice for people. When we feel we are being asked to choose a person over our set of beliefs or assumptions, our sense of conflict forces us to sort out where we focus our love. Do we love our values more than we love people?

A few Gospel stories tell of times when Jesus took on these nuanced assumptions in what I gently refer to as "intentional conflicts." Some of the stories take place on the Sabbath, the day reserved for rest, a day on which work is forbidden. A typical version of the story includes Jesus healing someone, followed by public outrage. Religious leaders voice disapproval, demanding that healings be scheduled for the other six days of the week. The institution of the Sabbath must be honored. Compelled by compassion, Jesus said, "The Sabbath was made for people, not people for the Sabbath" (Mark 2:27).

Institutions are notorious for putting their notions of community, even their versions of what behaviors are acceptable, ahead of the inclusion of people. We make the mistake of assuming that well-behaved people are the cogs in the machinery of our institutions rather than affirming that communities are at their best when made up of broken and wounded people.

I imagine that most of us think we love people more than a belief system or conduct standards, but the truth may be harder to swallow than we're prepared for. The saying "Hate the sin, not the sinner" only aggravates the conflict, pinning people against values, beliefs, and behaviors. I mean, really—hate the sin, not the sinner? What we're not so subtly doing when we lean into a statement like that is committing violence against human identity, a violence expressed in two ways.

First, if we adhere to a version of a doctrine of "original sin" that suggests that all of humanity can't help but do wrong, we tend to overidentify people with what they do by reducing all of humanity to sinners. If we make that damaging assumption, we can't help but assume that everything people do ultimately comes from a broken or wounded place of sinfulness.

Second, if we assume that nothing good can come from humanity because of our sinfulness, the "hate the sin" part basically applies to everything that any of us does—even our best attempts at doing good.

One of the problems with these views is that in the creation story God actually calls humanity "very good." So when we "hate the sin, not the sinner," we often are actually loving our perception of what is right, good, or just instead of loving one another. Not only do we love our own values in these scenarios, we are also declaring ourselves an authority on what we perceive to be "right." It's as if we're defending the institution of the Sabbath at the expense of the very people for whom the Sabbath was instituted.

> Institutions are notorious for putting their notions of community, even their versions of what behaviors are acceptable, ahead of the inclusion of people.

Is it ever okay to be exclusive? Do our values, convictions, or beliefs even matter in shaping our circles of friends or in forming our communities?

Reflecting on the example of Christ, we see that Jesus always offered himself but almost never imposed himself (inviting himself over to Zacchaeus's for dinner may be the lone exception). And in offering himself to all, Christ never shut himself off to anyone. In fact, Christ seemed so inclusive that he was accused of partying too much, drinking too much, and running around with the local riffraff.

On the other hand, Christ did hand-select his disciples. Some may argue that within a first-century Palestinian context (keeping in mind that Christ was religiously and culturally Jewish), the twelve guys Jesus called formed a fairly eclectic and diverse community. But if we're honest, there seems to be some sense of exclusion in terms of who Christ *didn't* include in his immediate community.

For those of us who are part of a church, an intentional community, or even a cause-driven collective of people united around common vocational goals, we have to recognize that staying true to our vision sometimes requires that we keep our circles tight.

After graduating from university, I immediately moved to India and helped start what we understand to be the first pediatric AIDS care home in South Asia. We had only enough rooms and beds for thirty or so children in the home, but every week someone would show up at our door with an abandoned child or a malnourished baby, pleading with us to take the child and give her or him a home.

Truth be told, I'm a bit of a sucker, and if it had been up to me, I would have given almost every one of those children a bed in the home. But had we taken in every kid who arrived at our door, we wouldn't have had room for children whose parents had died because of AIDS or kids who were HIV-positive themselves. Without other options in the city, we needed to protect the space we had created for that most underserved and desperate population of children.

One especially traumatic afternoon, we had turned away a child from a nearby slum whose young mother stood at our door with desperation in her eyes. I could hardly stand to look back at her, knowing we'd not be able to care for her child. Noticing how troubled I was, our Indian director, Patrick Samuel, sat with me and reminded me that the hardest part of having a vision is staying within the parameters of it.

Now, to the credit of Patrick and his wife, Victoria, they always found an alternative for those we were not able to take in. Their "no" was never really an absolute "no." Every time someone showed up with a vulnerable child, Patrick and Victoria would welcome them into the home, prepare a cup of coffee or tea for them, and then listen to their guest. If the child wasn't one we could admit, Patrick or Victoria would make as many calls as necessary to find another home or center that would accept the little one. One summer, I remember them making almost seventy referrals, finding homes for kids that we couldn't take in ourselves.

Typically these kinds of exclusionary stands don't make corresponding opportunities for inclusion. This comes back to the misappropriation of where we focus our energy toward love.

Not taking in every child who knocked on our door was actually *for* the inclusion of those on the margins, an option made for the most vulnerable of a community that had already excluded them. Sometimes it may appear that we need to be exclusive, but in such cases the only legitimate justification for any exclusionary stand would have to be to take an intentionally inclusive stand for those who are most rejected or excluded.

> The real danger of exclusion in community comes when we exclude the so-called other based on the fact that he or she is different.

The real danger of exclusion in community isn't when we're struggling to make stabilizing commitments based on our limitations but when we exclude the so-called other based on the fact that she or he is different.

Racism, heterosexism, denominationalism, and the hangovers of patriarchy continue to keep our communities fractured and insulated. Usually these are unconscious motivations that sneak up on us. Those of us who were culturally socialized as children naturally continue to replicate the kinds of communities we grew up in. It takes an awakening before many of us can work toward reimagining the beauty of what inclusive communities can become.

ECUMENICAL MUTINY

For years, my community unknowingly suffered from isolation. We were made up predominantly of white evangelical (actually, Wesleyan Arminian with a dash of the good old Holiness tradition) men. We didn't even notice. It took four or five years for women to outnumber men in the community and then another four or five years for women to become a substantial majority. We even had one year when our Omaha community sent a card out, proudly displaying a group photo on the front. An Asian-American friend picked the card up and, staring at the photograph, commented, "I'm so surprised that you're all white."

The Book of Revelation tells us that in paradise "every race and tongue, of every people and nation" will worship together (Revelation 5:9). In nearly every other aspect of life, we usually start with the end in sight. However, as we build communities we often forget that we are eternally being drawn to the culmination of inclusion. The indicators of what paradise may entail are the existential hopes that all humanity can be reconciled, that we can find wholeness tucked within the embrace of the divine. Sadly, we forget the urgency of this while living toward our eternal hopes.

One of the places we typically see a fractured community is

within our own Christian faith traditions. For many Christians, especially evangelicals, ecumenism is a concept we react against. To too many, inclusion implies liberalizing our faith communities through compromise. It's a common misunderstanding that ecumenical unity dilutes the commitment to the values and truth found in Scripture.

Our community refers to ecumenism not as moving *away* from values and our perceptions of truth for the sake of unity but as moving *toward* the center: Christ. When Catholic, Orthodox, and Protestant Christians can come together in the name of Jesus, we see signs of restoration in the body of Christ. If we in the church are a fractured and segmented body, how will the world know we are God's but by our love for one another (John 13:31–35)?

We encountered our first experiences with a form of ecclesiological mutiny when Josh, one of our community members in India, started dating a woman who was Catholic. In the safety of their relationship, he started questioning some of the teachings from his Protestant upbringing. We were old friends, had grown up in the same town, and had enough history to create open, honest dialogue and, at times, fair fights.

As a former Catholic myself, I was well versed in arguments against Catholicism. I remember emailing back and forth, sending pointed questions that really did more to draw deeper lines between Catholicism and Protestant evangelicalism than to provide authentic ways for both of us to find our way closer to Christ.

In the end, Josh joined the Catholic Church. Around that time another of our staff members, Kyle, also started dating a

woman who was Catholic. They got married. He remained Protestant; she remained Catholic.

A few years later, Phileena began considering the Catholic
Church. It made sense. We'd pitched tons of Henri Nouwen
books around the community, and, truth be told, he is easily
one of the best spirituality authors of our age. Phileena and I
had also spent quite a bit of time with Mother Teresa and the
Missionaries of Charity. If you'd been with them, you understand how beautifully they lived their faith. Phileena had exposure to and mentoring by Father Thomas Keating and a ten-day
silent retreat at his monastery. Together we had made pilgrim-
ages to Assisi, Italy, and Santiago, Spain. When Phileena joined
the Catholic Church, I got the "margin call on her soul" (as I
put it) from her concerned family. We lost a lot of financial
support, even from some of our longest-standing friends.

Fears simmered throughout our community, stoking urgent
questions: What will this do to us? Does this compromise our
theological integrity? Will an ecclesial unraveling begin, and will
we be able to stop it? How will this divide us?

Surprisingly, nothing changed. In fact, we actually became
stronger because of the presence of a few Catholics in our community. All of the externalized theological abstractions remained
on a conceptual level. The only hurdle we really experienced
was at the communion table. Though significant, the challenges
around the Eucharist were not enough to keep us from our love
for one another. This painful place of separation also led us to
pray more thoughtfully for the unity of the church.

Other than that, our community carried on, and our relationships and friendships continued to grow. We now look for

theological diversity and consider ecumenism a core value and guiding principle in forming community. Funny how things have changed.

We've learned that if we're going to be the people of God, we have to embrace a broad range of ecclesial diversity while simultaneously creating a stronger sense of theological unity.

Over the years, we have stumbled into a few affirmations, or community confessions. They're basic and almost painfully obvious, but they have held us together: Christ is the head of these Christian faith traditions, and our love for Christ unites us in community and compels us in service. We affirm that our Christian identity is rooted in Christ, while recognizing that we can't separate Christ from tradition or we will perpetuate the Protestant tendency of rejecting other traditions. This can be difficult because some of us have overidentified our Christianity with versions of Protestantism or Catholicism.

> Henri Nouwen is easily one of the best spirituality authors of our age.

We confess the tendency toward reductionism in our doctrine that creates holes in our Christian faith traditions. The theological continuity of the church can't be rejected by our stubborn ecclesiologies.

We seek to embody our hope for unity. Is our church an institution or a community? Reorienting ourselves around the person of Jesus and the community, we affirm that the Spirit of God forms us around our shared love for Christ. We have redefined our community around the church's center, not its denominational fragments.

When we talk about ecumenism, we're not suggesting that

we all should figuratively grab the central flagpole of Christ with one hand and then be allowed to reach out as liberally as we can with the other, just so we have one hand still holding on to our traditional or conservative roots. Rather, we recognize that all of us are at different places on the margins and within the embrace of our Christian identities. It's just that our aim is toward Christ as the center, and that is our collective trajectory.

Truth be told, in our community we have several different perspectives about all of this. North Americans sometimes seem to be much less concerned about letting doctrine draw lines than our South American or Asian community members are—for reasons perhaps cultural, possibly modern/postmodern collisional, maybe even generational.

It's not been easy.

These kinds of sensibilities, though gaining broader acceptance in Christian communities, can still become divisive.

> Our aim is toward Christ as the center, and that is our collective trajectory.

Within this shifting ecumenical incubator of our Christian imagination, we have found that vocationally it is easy to bring churches and Christians together around things we know and believe to be true; we can all agree, for instance, that God doesn't want children sexually exploited and commodified in the commercial sex industry. Discovering theological unity in that tragic space is easy. So we stay in those obvious places and inch our way closer to one another based on what else we can agree on. We do this rather than highlighting and overidentifying the so-called other by what separates us.

Throughout the Gospels, Christ attempts to form a community that doesn't exclude deeply committed religious people, including the Pharisees and Sadducees. They do a fine job of excluding themselves. Rather, Christ looks for common ground as a hinge to community, even tucking voices on the fringes into the company of his message bearers.

So when we affirm these places of unity, I am convinced the world will know we belong to Christ by the prophetic eruption of our love for one another. Until then, the divisions and fractured body we've become stand as an indictment against ourselves only.

Remember the beautiful prayer rug in the Romanian chapel? If it had been woven from a single thread, it wouldn't have been nearly as beautiful. Truly beautiful communities are polychromatic.

THE BABY MADE WHOLE

While on pilgrimage in Spain, Phileena and I fought our way through a violent windstorm. Birds flying overhead flapped their wings furiously, only to be blown backward. As we leaned into the stiff resistance, fighting for every step, forceful gusts of wind got the best of us.

Exhausted by the effort, we stopped at an empty cathedral in a quaint Basque village. The church, full of art and precious religious relics, was strikingly lonely. That spring morning Phileena and I were the only ones there. In the emptiness of that sacred museum I marveled at the apparent disrespect reflected for many of my friends who live and die in poverty. Could this place of worship, along with the thousands like it worldwide, really be in honor of the Christ who had no place to rest his head? Just the value of the gold leaf alone could provide clean drinking water for many of my friends, whose polluted water keeps their children perpetually sick.

Sitting there, I was reminded of the maternity dispute King Solomon was asked to resolve. The third chapter of 1 Kings tells of a child fought over by two women, both claiming to be the infant's mother. Solomon shrewdly ordered that the baby be cut in two pieces so each of the quarreling women could have part of the newborn. But at that verdict, the true mother was made evident when she insisted that the baby be given to the other woman rather than allowing it to be killed.

> Our challenge is to find reconciliatory ways where wholeness can be celebrated.

Laced with imagery, the story pops with allegory. A vulnerable baby is a metaphor for Christ, who was constantly a target for violence. The "un-mother" emerges as a fractured symbol of the church—an unfaithful and cantankerous bride. A looming sword, the vivid image of what divides our competing and divisive versions of Christ that make some Christian faith traditions seemingly imcompatible.

Too often it appears the un-mother is still among us, causing division in selfish pursuit of having her way. That baby, or the claims to our perceptions of Jesus, are still being fought over by two mothers—be it those who are poor and the nonpoor; egalitarian women and complementarian men; competing faith traditions; gays or lesbians and heterosexuals; whites and people of color. Given the opportunity to determine the true mother of this child, the divided church continues to demand the mutilation of the baby.

Our challenge is to find reconciliatory ways where wholeness can be celebrated, marrying memory and community, healing the wounds our division has caused our communities—and subsequently Christ.

Transition

Thirty Letters and a Box of Wooden Planks

[The one] who loves [her] dream of a community more than the Christian community itself becomes a destroyer of the latter.

— Dietrich Bonhoeffer

Transitions have something addictive about them, something sexy. There's something profoundly interesting about "what's next." Transitions are an inevitable part of community, but how they are handled has as much power over the sustainability of a community as just about anything else.

As my community prepared to celebrate its anniversary, we reflected on the failures of how we have handled some of our own transitions. During our first twenty years a lot of imaginative things happened. We certainly had plenty to celebrate. But before we spent a whole lot of time patting ourselves on the back or looking and dreaming into the future, we realized that we first needed to look back on our past. In doing so, we found much to lament.

Rather than ramp up a huge campaign to commodify our twentieth anniversary or use the momentum around our celebration to recruit new staff or launch new programming, we attempted to organize our first alumni association. We called it our "Continuity Community" in an effort to affirm that those who had gone on were still central to our collective identity, that in many ways we figuratively stand on their shoulders.

We chased down the names and addresses of everyone who had served on our board, worked full-time or part-time, or had interned at any of our sites. Of the several hundred names, at least thirty folks had left deeply wounded and had been hurt by how their departures had been handled.

> Before we celebrated the present or anticipated the future, we first needed to look back on our past.

Thirty out of several hundred doesn't seem too bad, but they were thirty former friends, companions, and community members. Their feelings of disenfranchisement or woundedness had fostered a collection of broken relationships that created pain for many of us.

I began meeting for coffee with one of those dear friends who had experienced an unpleasant transition from our community. Jared had worked with us for almost ten years. He had been a key figure in the success of more than one of our international communities. Around the table, we talked through his pain of leaving the community. He'd encountered some awful misunderstandings that had been aggravated by my response to his decision to leave. That had made his transition regrettably challenging.

Meeting with him was hard work and required a lot of vulnerability and honesty. I apologized for many things, things I didn't know I had done, as well as plenty of things in which I knew I'd been complicit. He graciously accepted the apologies and extended forgiveness.

That time with Jared spent around the table drinking coffee was practice for what would become months of painful and difficult conversations. They gave me the courage for my next attempt to reconcile our community's mishandled transitions.

It started with thirty letters, each to one of the thirty disenfranchised former members of our community. The letters started with words of gratitude for the person's participation in our community. I affirmed their sacrifices and contributions, highlighting the ways they had helped us become what we were now. We wouldn't have had a twentieth anniversary to celebrate if it hadn't been for their hard work, and I wanted them to know that.

I also addressed personal and specific ways in which their transitions had been mismanaged, which meant I spent days trying to get each letter right. I apologized that we hadn't always handled our staff transitions as well as we should have. I asked for forgiveness for not supporting people well in those crucial days of uncertainty. I said I was sorry for the ways some people had felt blamed by the community when they had left and the fact that some folks had been made to feel as if they had abandoned us. Finally, I confessed that we sometimes put unfair pressure and unrealistic expectations on people to be more for our community—pressure and expectations beyond what anyone could deliver.

It was tough writing those letters. And then I had to mail them. Once they were posted, I waited and wondered. Would anyone respond? Were there wrongs I had forgotten?

After a few weeks, the responses started trickling in. Calls, emails, Facebook messages, and lots of handwritten letters made their way back to me—for almost eight months.

The handwritten letters were the most emotional. They were the longest, and usually they were the most honest. There were handwritten notes with bold lettering and thick lines indicating that a pen had been pressed deeply into the paper. The feelings expressed in many of those letters bled into the paper and popped off the pages. The letters were the crack in the door for reconnections: most of them led to long phone calls, meals, and face-to-face meetings that nurtured space for reconciliation and healing.

I left some of the meetings feeling pretty beat up, and some of that I deserved. Many days I came home exhausted. Some conversations were filled with angry exchanges, while others led to a series of tearful confessions from both sides. Finally, though, I'd made contact with almost everyone.

> Navigating transitions is one of the most significant and constant struggles a community will face.

What did I learn from all this? One of the many things was that we had actually handled the transitions even worse than I'd thought. I learned that a community, just like a person, carries a huge potential to wound people. Sure, lots of it had been unintentional, and for the most part, we didn't even know what we were doing or had done. But that didn't change how those making transitions experienced the situation.

Transitions are natural and inevitable in all communities. Yes, there will almost inevitably come a time when we know, or our community knows, that it's time to go. Navigating transitions is one of the most significant and constant struggles a community will face. But what if most of our reasons for going are bad reasons? What if we could learn to see struggles and dissonance as reasons to stay? What could those unexpected and unlikely gifts possibly be?

Reflecting on our failures helps us avoid repeating mistakes. In a perfect world, these processes would flow smoothly, but once one person's humanity collides with another's, we don't always handle things well. These kinds of difficult situations in our communities can sometimes aggravate what is already a difficult journey.

When it's time for someone to go, that person is usually the first to know. Of course, situations arise when the community may discern this before the individual, but once a person comes to this conclusion, is there a constructive way to submit it back to the community for collective discernment?

Discerning the answers to the hard questions can be the loneliest places we find ourselves. Such questions as What should I do when:

I want to go?

I need to leave a community?

I want to move on from a relationship?

Even confessing our desire to leave can come across as a form of abandonment or self-centeredness. When exploring the implications of transitions, we risk being misunderstood. And the repeated misunderstanding of seeing how others' transitions are mishandled sometimes creates a fear that it will happen to us. And so a cycle is created where transitions are announced rather than processed with a community.

I honestly don't believe that any community will handle every single one of its transitions with grace. In light of our humanity, it's a given that there will be someone who will leave a community hurt, misunderstood, or feeling unsupported. This is one of the tricky dynamics of building community. But the key is to embrace the truth that we're all responsible for how we, as individuals, transition and how we, as a community, handle those transitions. When we do that well, things on the other side of moving on can be better and relationships don't have to be sacrificed.

What's really sad about this reaching-back practice of reconciliation is that you have to do it over and over. When I became the director of my community, the first five years of our community's life were marked by a trail of broken and hurt people. The hurts were almost entirely unintentional but nonetheless real. So not only did I write letters at our twentieth year, but I had done it fifteen years earlier as well. Oh, the irony of repeating our mistakes. The pain of seeing cycles of brokenness played out in community was devastating for me. And, in many ways, it still is.

I should have learned; *we* should have learned. But simply recognizing the inevitability of community transitions doesn't mean we handle them better. The only way that happens is to be thoughtful, intentional, and honest as we work through transitions.

Dealing well with transitions requires that we develop the emotional and relational tools to negotiate and handle these very sensitive rhythms in the life of a community. Avoiding blame, not picking sides, speaking honorably of the communities we leave or the people who transition from our community are all parts of a bigger process—one that must also include space for grieving and room for celebrating.

Writing those letters around our community's twentieth anniversary wasn't a success story in reconciling broken relationships and mishandled transitions; it was actually the repetition of a failure. Even after all those years, we had yet to learn how to hold one another in the vulnerable and sensitive periods of transitions.

Unless communities learn that—until we obtain the tools and then approach transitions with openness, humility, and grace—we will continue to perpetuate broken relationships, fractured community, and an inability to transition people into a community without suspicion and resentments waiting to happen.

WHEN EVERYTHING COMES CRASHING DOWN

Dreaming about the future, making inside jokes, finishing each other's sentences, having late-night conversations that seem as though they could go on forever, taking snapshots and photographs to preserve memories, sharing favorite music and films, resting in the possibilities of what's to come—at the beginning of all great friendships or new community connections, it seems as though those things will never end. But to our surprise, many of them do.

Transitions are hard, sometimes the most difficult of all human experiences. Transitions are inevitable but almost never anticipated. Transitions never seem to happen at a good time.

Remember the game Jenga? It's a box of little wooden planks that are used to build a tower. Back and forth, you and your opponent push and pull the wooden planks out of the tower while trying to keep it balanced. The idea is to create enough instability with the blocks you remove such that one of the blocks your opponent removes topples the tower.

Jenga is a lot like the collection of friendships and relationships we compile over the course of our lifetime. Sometimes the loss of a particular friendship is the Jenga of them all: once that relationship is lost, all the others come crashing down around it. Ask anyone who's gone through a divorce about this. They'll tell you the grief of how the separating of lives once woven together tears lifelong friendships apart.

> Even when transitions in our relationships are necessary, they aren't easy.

Even when transitions in our relationships are necessary, they aren't easy. Though hard decisions sometimes have to be made, the decisions and subsequent transitions don't reduce the impact, nor do they scrub the pain away.

Moving on is never easy, and even when these kinds of decisions are made, it sometimes seems as though the conversations are never closed. "What ifs" and "remember whens" are sprinkled into conversations, prodding at nostalgia and regret. Painful reminders erupt when you're not invited to a wedding or a dinner party or when someone who always used to call on your birthday is silent or absent.

When you've invested in a relationship that undergoes a transition, even one that is necessary, processing the adjustments gets harder and harder over time. Haunting memories cause new kinds of loneliness.

PROCESSING THE INEVITABILITY
OF TRANSITIONS

Transitions always have a reason, be they justifiable or short-sighted. When we refuse to validate someone's intentions for her or his transition, we make things worse. In what is often a bad situation, either we can aggravate things by fighting or we can extend grace. On the other side of departures from relationships, either people are embittered and any possibility of a reconnect or reconciliation is lost, or they have an openness to return to or redefine a relationship.

It takes courage to try to understand the reasons for transitions; understanding, or at least attempting to do so, goes a long way to salvage what is left. But we must realize that trying to understand may not mean that understanding occurs. The attempt is the goal, not always understanding itself.

This is demonstrated in a willingness to listen without judgment, even if we don't understand or agree. Sometimes it's a phase of life, a change in career, family issues, or even personal growth awakenings that necessitate transitions. All these things can change people in ways that force them to make changes in their social circles. Phase-of-life transitions are normal and should be expected. Sometimes transitions happen at a time that feels incompatible with the rest of the community—things such as an unexpected pregnancy or a surprise engagement often move a community's timeline, forcing everyone to adjust.

A good friend once told me that folks who stay committed to the same partner are actually married to four or five different people during their lifetime. I can attest to that. The person I am today would probably never have married the person Phileena was when I first met her. We've both changed so much that we might not even recognize versions of ourselves from college. The man I was then would look at the more progressive version of the person I've now become with judgment, suspicion, and a lack of tolerance. And the person I am now would find the university version of myself very narrow-minded, naive, and sheltered. Life has a way of beating us into new versions of ourselves. These emerging versions of self, when dynamic and open to change, can't always stay in communities or relationships that once supported us but now may stifle our growth.

During various phases and periods of growth we often discover new ways of expressing our vocations. Vocational illumination or redirection can sometimes feel like a critique of the existing communities or relationships we are in. When we change jobs, move from one worshipping community to another, grow in personal understanding of how to live faithful to our life experience and new opportunities, we have to be careful to recognize the impact it has on those closest to us. Just because we change jobs doesn't mean we've become a different person. Often, our core vocation stays the same but sadly isn't affirmed by those who stay.

Finally, sometimes the reasons for our own transitions or the transitions of those in our lives and communities are due to very real limitations or failures in our existing circle of relationships. This can be very difficult for everyone to admit. But we are human, and we won't always get things right.

ELIMINATING THE CULTURE OF BLAME

When people transition from friendships, relationships, and especially communities, there is a tendency to blame others. Moving on is hard, especially when we won't let ourselves or when we feel as though we're not free to move on. The natural defense mechanism then is blame.

People are blamed for leaving. People who leave often blame others for why they feel they must go. *Someone* has to be at fault for a transition, which ultimately leads to painful breakdowns in relationships. Blaming is easy. But it also uncovers emotional immaturity and lacks honesty. When we blame, we expose our own loss of control over a scenario. Blaming rests on the subtext that things happening around us are the fault of others.

> People who are emotionally healthy can recognize their own roles in the scripts of their lives.

People who are emotionally healthy can recognize their own roles in the scripts of their lives. But those who aren't tend to blame others. Blaming others may feel like self-protection, but it actually hinders our ability to learn and grow and prevents getting to the legitimate reasons why transitions are necessary.

Blaming also tends to rewrite the past. People start friendships or join communities for clear reasons. People who give themselves to relationships are the best advocates of and champions for those they bond with. But let a transition happen, and they often become the fiercest critic of what they've left. Former Catholics seem to be the hardest on Catholicism. People who've left any church, for that matter, usually have a long list of the reasons why they left. Though at one point they might have been the best advocate for their church, in transition they become the most critical of it.

A transition is felt not just by the person leaving but also by those staying behind. Both parties have legitimate experiences of transition. Many times, those who stay behind experience a transition as betrayal. This can happen when someone in the midst of a transition isn't given space to process the motivations and implications of why it was time to go.

Creating a safe space for a redefinition of self and a rediscovery of vocation in the midst of a transition is necessary for everyone involved. A community on the other side of a transition needs to be able to reorient itself and adjust to the pain of loss. People leaving a community usually need a clean break to step back and rediscover who they are when the way they express their vocation changes. When the transitional space isn't handled gently, it can lead to perpetual separation, something that almost no one wants.

What's tricky about the need for space in times of transition is that it's usually misunderstood. People who've been so committed and engaged in their community sometimes don't know who they are apart from it. On the other side of a transition, they may need to catch their breath, to take a step back and recalibrate their personal view of self. This is important, and providing this space, though difficult, creates the potential for relationships to be salvaged.

But when people who've moved on from a community take this space, rather than working it through with the community, the distance can feel like abandonment for those who stay—which too often turns into a nasty cycle of misunderstanding and further estrangement.

Working together is key. When the need for transition arises, having both individuals and a community attempt to understand the whys of the transition and create a culture of honoring one another rather than blaming one another is difficult to learn and do. But it is vital to healthy community and, in the long run, will minimize the potential for fallout and unintended isolation that often accompanies transitions.

WHEN IT'S TIME TO GO

A few years ago, Tim, a Dutch Reformed pastor and dear friend, passed along the document his church used to help people leave that congregation. The title of that short paper was "When It's Time to Go," and, though a bit overly suggestive, the content was practical and thoughtful.

Our community reviewed this paper, reflected on it, and revised it into a thorough vocational discernment process that we now include in our new-staff orientation materials. Our version is called "Community and Transitions."

As much as we try to prepare a person and the community for transition, sometimes people still mentally and relationally check out long before their last day in a particular community. Sometimes this is an important part of the transitional process; other times it creates an environment that becomes toxic. This can be true even when the transition is one that obviously needs to happen for the health of the community member, the community she or he is leaving, or both.

Typically, when people overidentify who

> Handling the phases of transition when it's time to go can be harder than arriving at the decision to leave.

they are with their community, there inevitably comes a time of differentiation. Usually this takes place when someone transitions out of a community, though it can also happen with people while they remain in the community. Even if the transition (or awakening to a healthy differentiated sense of self) is for good reasons and handled well, there is still a series of phases that needs to be lived and experienced.

Handling the phases of transition when it's time to go can be harder than arriving at the decision to leave.

PHASES OF TRANSITIONAL AWAKENING

Phases of transitional awakening sometimes happen almost immediately after a community departure, while some don't kick in until years later. Usually though, people who leave a community need a clean break and some safe space to renegotiate who they are apart from their former community. The following phases often accompany this break:

Grief. This first phase is a common and predictable experience when anyone faces a major life or relational transition. When one has participated in the routines and rhythms of a community, the group experiences a kind of muscle memory of security. Saying good-bye to the safety of rhythms, the incubator of community, and the inevitable redefining of relationships often introduces a much-needed period of honest grieving.

Romanticism. Sometimes a period of romanticism follows transition when people are not able to grieve. It's as if their inability to be honest in grief causes them to be dishonest in how they remember things.

I thought no church could be better than the Omaha church in which I grew up. In my years at university I remained disconnected and restless, always looking for a worshipping community that might be as good as the one back home. I must have been so annoying, romanticizing something so human and beautifully flawed.

Moving from a deeply satisfying and meaningful community experience into something new, different, or strange can create an illusion regarding how good things were in a former community. It's not bad to look back on an old community with appreciation, but romanticizing how things "used to be" can lead to deeper grief or even a profound sense of dissatisfaction in one's new community.

Though some romanticized visions of a former community may be accurate, many are unrealistic and actually point to significant phases-of-life movements. We see this a lot in our community. It's a common occurrence for recent graduates who experienced satisfying student-life communities on their campuses or at their universities. I actually was quite frightened by the advice one of my college mentors gave me as my own graduation approached: "Make the most of your college experience; these will be the best days of your life."

Whoa. I loved being a student but had actually hoped things would get better and better the older I got.

Correction. Eventually there is a phase of correction as people process their romanticism. Grieving the loss of what was comforting in community and subsequently romanticizing our memories cannot be sustained. Realism sets in.

When I moved from Nebraska to Kentucky to go to university, I missed my home church—a lot. And I talked about that church ad nauseam to my friends. In my mind, that church was as close to perfect as any church could be. It took a few years of being away for me to come to terms with the reality that every church is made up of flawed humans who, though they are trying their best, aren't actually perfect. Correcting our romanticism is a practice of truth telling, of being honest with others and ourselves.

When a community has a healthy postcorrection transitional process—one that includes healthy grieving, fond remembering, and honest renegotiations regarding imbalances in perception—former community members become some of its best champions and advocates.

The flip side isn't so pretty. When people aren't given the freedom to grieve or don't find the courage to legitimately process their transition, the outcome of their moving on is usually sharp criticism. This is important and can be entirely fair, because someone who has actually participated in a community has the potential to be its greatest advocate as well as its fiercest critic. And that can be another phase in transitional awareness.

Criticism. Former community members may need to learn how to honestly critique a community they have overly romanticized or idealized. This can bring wholeness to an individual's community experience when she isn't malicious or mean-spirited in her assessment.

Sometimes a former community member may feel he needs to level criticism against the group he's left to convince himself that he is justified in leaving. This sort of self-justification can be very damaging to relationships with current community members. We need to be careful that our transitions are as healthy as possible and do as little damage to the potential future of friendships we hope to retain.

Sometimes a former community member uses criticism as a proxy for processing other parts of her life. Her former boss or pastor can become a target for unresolved authority issues or parent wounds or disappointments with religious organizations. Or perhaps her former community becomes a symbol of anything wrong with her perceptions or disappointments about community life.

> When a community has a healthy postcorrection transitional process, former community members become some of its best champions and advocates.

FACILITATING THE PHASES

In recent years, we have begun routine debriefings for everyone who leaves our community. These conversations help people unpack their experiences objectively and in many instances help them rescript their transitions with better accuracy.

When former community members become critical, other former community members sometimes gravitate to them. Though space for reflection can create a safe environment for support and processing, disgruntled former community members find themselves being fused together by critical and cynical conversations. Sadly, this usually breeds a new kind of toxic community.

Until a person really grieves his transition, detaches and

disconnects in healthy and positive ways, and then reconnects where appropriate, he may not have the clarity of perspective to make honest critiques of his former community. Other times, such conversations are self-soothing or coping mechanisms necessary to deal with his or her unresolved grief about having left a community that once meant so much to them.

In most of our own community transitions, we've seen habitual patterns that lead to failure or success. When someone leaves badly, she has a harder time making her next connection a positive and lasting one. But if she transitions well, she is able to carry forward the gifts of her former community into her next one.

WHEN TRANSITIONS CAN'T BE RESOLVED

Sometimes, no matter how hard we try to make a transition smooth and honoring, things end badly. Inevitably, there will be times when someone isn't ready to go but needs to leave. Sometimes differences can't be ironed out, and our best attempts at understanding will still come up lacking. And if we're honest, there will be times when everyone involved in a transition contributes to the painful messiness of it not being handled well.

> When someone leaves badly, she has a harder time making her next connection a positive and lasting one.

In these instances it's still important to honor the process. When we purposely put our differences aside and choose not to speak negatively of a transitioned community member or a former community, it goes a long way toward a possible future of reconciliation. If a transition has already been mishandled, speaking unfavorably about the community or person will only further aggravate the pain and delay any possible reconciliation.

When someone leaves hurt or upset, it's likely that he may speak critically of the community he's left. Perhaps he needs to justify his departure by naming the reasons for his transition, or he may feel a need to be justified. Whatever the case, the community taking a defensive posture or trying to protect its reputation almost always backfires. If the members of a community have done everything they can to make a transition as smooth as possible, that's the best defense. And usually it's a good idea to let our friends defend us rather than trying to defend ourselves.

Together, we can do better. We can learn to love even in our disagreements and differences. We can hope that when a resolution seems impossible, there's always a chance. And that chance for restoration is largely dependent on our doing everything we can to keep the doors of communication patiently open, others' reputations untarnished, and invitations for appropriate reconnections standing.

> **Transitions handled well lead to stability.**

THE UNEXPECTED GIFT OF TRANSITIONS

Transitions are important and can actually be quite healthy for communities. The solutions to the problems connected to bad transitions should never lead to transitionless communities but to greater opportunities to act with honor and respect.

Communities will fail and community members will, too, but

it doesn't have to be a devastating experience. Handling transitions well allows us to live beyond the pain and through the messiness of our community's inevitable and natural rhythms. It helps us learn to celebrate transitions, receive them as gifts, and facilitate them in ways that the warren of Jenga-stacked friendships doesn't come crashing down. And ultimately, transitions handled well lead to stability.

6

The Unknown Self

The Search for Suti Sana

As long as our life and our work together are based on a false
or distorted self-understanding, we are bound to become
entangled in interpersonal conflicts and lose perspective on
our common task.

—Henri Nouwen

Q uite a few therapists stay in business because many of us are
on a perpetually unresolved journey of self-discovery. A lifetime's worth of experiences would seem to lead to clarity about
who we are and how we perceive ourselves, but what usually
happens is that our subconscious sees the fuzziest versions of
who we really are. We get caught up in self-imaging our identities based on the trauma we've experienced or the successes and
accomplishments we've attained. Sometimes we cling to false
versions of ourself as sincere and earnest attempts to understand
who we are.

But these dangerous paths to self-discovery usually lead us
further away from the truth of who we truly are. A friend of
mine, Blanca, has taught me as much about this as anyone.

• • •

As a child, Blanca could never have imagined, even in her worst nightmares, how her life would turn out.

Blanca was born in Chile; her father passed away when she was very young. Forced to grow up with a stepfather, she was just seven when the abuse started. He sexually assaulted, molested, and raped her. Then came physical abuse and threats. She endured the torment for several years, until she finally found courage to reach out for help from her mother. But Blanca's mother failed to protect her daughter, siding with her partner. Hurt, Blanca wanted freedom. At fifteen, she finally escaped by running away.

Blanca made new friends, who suggested that she consider leaving the country to earn more money where the work was better. With nothing to lose, she agreed. Still a child, she was too naive to suspect that anything was amiss. So she followed her friends to Peru.

They abandoned her at a brothel.

It was a typical scam used by many human traffickers: offer a job as a waitress to draw the girl in. But what happened to Blanca was beyond any imagining.

She was taken to a small border town in Peru and sold to a pimp. To her surprise, she recognized many of the young girls working in the brothel; they were from her village in Chile.

Her first night in the bar, someone referred to her as the "new girl." A curious customer overheard and called Blanca over to the table where he sat. Still thinking she was waitressing, she attempted to take his order. He asked her to sit with him. During their conversation he put his hand on her knee and began groping her leg. Disgusted, she jumped up, yelled at the man, and stormed off. But to her horror, she was forced to go to a room with him, where he coerced her to remove her clothes.

Somehow that night and for her first week in the brothel, Blanca managed to avoid any sexual contact. But like all people victimized by the commercial sex industry, her captors did eventually "break her in." Violent threats, unspeakable torture, and repeated rapes crushed her spirit.

Her resolve and determination died.

Forced into prostitution, Blanca worked every day, often having sex with as many as thirty to forty men a night. When she was sixteen, she gave birth to her first baby, who died a month later. She eventually became so ill that she couldn't work, so she was thrown out of the brothel. In the following years she moved from one abusive relationship to another, intermittently returning to the brothels, where she felt protected and provided for. Finally she turned to alcohol and violence, sometimes even stabbing the men who were using her for sex.

In the brokenness of her tender heart, she longed to return home, to fall into the arms of the mother who had betrayed her.

During an almost forty-year career in the commercial sex industry, Blanca moved from brothel to brothel across Peru and was eventually brought to Bolivia. Worn out, she ended up in El Alto, near La Paz, the end of the line for women in prostitution. This is where women who are older, and often considered less attractive, go to work.

El Alto is one of the fastest-growing and poorest cities in South America. The slum

> **In the brokenness of her tender heart, she longed to return home, to fall into the arms of the mother who had betrayed her.**

overgrowth of La Paz began creeping up the hills around the city, spilling out onto the plains below the Andes Mountains. A giant slum turned city, El Alto now has nearly 1 million inhabitants, of whom the average age is sixteen years old. With a staggering illiteracy rate of 78 percent aggravated by chronic undernourishment and unemployment, for some women prostitution is the only option for income.

The commercial sex industry in El Alto is supported by a large "volunteer" force due to the lack of adequate jobs in the city, but women trafficked from places such as Argentina, Chile, Brazil, and Peru also fill brothel rooms. Women working in the brothels turn tricks for as little as two dollars per customer, and half of that goes to the house. Most women spend their days at home with their children and families, working nights until they've met with a minimum of ten clients; others see as many as thirty or forty (or more) men a day.

At fifty-two, Blanca had worked for as long as her body and soul could handle. With less and less clientele to sustain her income and a deep desire to leave the industry, she began selling hot meals to the girls working in the brothels.

In 2001, Andrea and Andy Baker joined our community and moved to El Alto. In time, a community quietly formed around them. Over the years, they've met hundreds of commercial sex workers in El Alto.

Including Blanca.

Blanca took a job as the Bakers' nanny and then eventually participated in a therapeutic program, Paso a Paso (Step by Step) held at the Casa de Esperanza (House of Hope) drop-in center for women in the sex

With those sacred words of Scripture, Blanca claimed a new identity and freedom.

trade. With the support of a loving community, Blanca finally found the safe space she needed to begin putting the pieces of her life back together.

Her childhood stolen, her sexuality plundered, Blanca grieved for the life she wished she'd had. Her family, the legal system, society, and even her community had all failed her. In the ashes of what was left of her life, Blanca called out to God for healing. The answer came in the sixty-second chapter of the book of Isaiah: "My God has answered me," or "Eliana."

With those sacred words of Scripture, Blanca claimed a new identity and freedom. Putting all of her pain and abuse behind her, she chose a new name: Eliana. The community received the gift of her new name and her new life and followed her toward freedom.

A new name.
A new life.
Renewed hope.

Eliana, the Bakers, and the rest of the community began dreaming of how to help other women out of the trade, how to help them recover and restore their lives. Together they helped launch Suti Sana. A combination of Aymara and Spanish, the prominent local languages, Suti Sana means "healed name." The women of Suti Sana are trained to make bags from *aguayos,* traditional Bolivian wool blankets. An aguayo is typically wrapped tightly around a woman's body and used to carry newborn babies or life-giving goods such as fruits, grains, and other foods. Making and selling these bags helps create freedom for those once enslaved in the sex industry.

Most of us won't be trafficked into the sex trade, but many of us allow our identities to be defined by someone else. Most of us may never experience anything remotely close to the life Eliana has lived, but friends like Eliana lead us to grace. She allows us to journey with her toward the new names God wants to give us. Blanca got a new name—Eliana—and many of us who've been mistreated, who have made mistakes and suffered the consequences of ours and others' failures, need to follow her to God's heart.

We too need a new name.

We need to learn to love ourselves. Some of us need to learn to love ourselves again. Others need to learn to do so for the first time.

KNOWING OUR TRUE SELVES

Who are we? What do we mean by identity? The work of Vinay Samuel and Chris Sugden offers helpful handles for understanding identity as it relates to dignity. Samuel and Sugden suggest that identity is "who we are," while dignity assumes "what we're worth."[1] For the greater part of my life I've tried to validate my worth (dignity) by developing a valuable projection of who I thought I needed to be (identity). I've avoided learning how to know my true self. Instead, I've pandered to thin versions of my false self.

I constantly wrestle with the question "Who am I?"

How can we nurture the unknown self toward an awakening to our true selves? Henri Nouwen suggests that we are the beloved sons and daughters of God. Pretty simple. But he gets to this landing point of illuminated identity by first dismantling the lies we allow our souls to listen to.

Nouwen suggests that most of us live in the unstable places of false identities that attempt to conform to illusionary suggestions such as "I am what I have," "I am what I do," and "I am what other people think about me."

Regrettably, I've spent much of my own life trying to compile memorable experiences, the "right" books for my library, an eclectic music collection, a balanced stock portfolio, beautiful art for my town house, and quite a few other things that somehow seem to make me feel a good bit happy about my life. Yet they're never enough, and the sense of happiness I think I experience actually just hollows me out even more, creating new kinds of dissatisfactions

> How can we nurture the unknown self toward an awakening to our true selves?

that propel me to chase down more stuff I don't really need. Sometimes I really do think "I am what I have."

A significant part of my job involves speaking at universities, conferences, student groups, and churches. Every so often when I nail a talk, I feel awesome. I sometimes overidentify myself with my successes. What's worse, though, or at least feels worse, is when I overidentify myself with failures. I can be pretty hard on myself. When I mess up a talk, I'll turn that failure over and over in my mind for days on end.

Far worse than messing up a talk is hurting a friend. When I fail someone in a relationship, I don't let myself off the hook. Sleepless nights are pretty common for me, many of them marked by replays of failures and missteps. Fortunately, most of my mistakes have landed me in the gracious arms of a community that accepts, forgives, and works to help redirect me. Stumbling forward. But there have been some pretty dark days of living in the lie "I am what I do."

Nouwen's third lie of the unknown self, "I am what others think of me," might be the toughest for me. I like to get reactions from people. I like to nudge people to consider thinking differently about things such as heterosexism, Islamophobia, environmental stewardship, the gender of God, patriarchy, and a long list of other conversations we all could use a bit more reflection on. But when I post something online that I know will elicit negative responses, the reactions still end up stinging a little when they come. People react and respond, sometimes judgmentally, even with personal attacks. What hurts is my ego, my false self, which begs for attention, affection, and approval. These urges are strong. They convolute the reality of who I really am by causing me to play to what others want me to be.

The three lies that Henri Nouwen outlined have illuminated my flawed identity.

Rather than resting in my belovedness and the truth that I bear, the imprint of the divine within me, I have tried my best to become someone, something significant. And herein lies the greatest irony: I have been reaching for significance, when the greatest significance of all was already present in my soul.

UNCOVERING OUR ORIGINAL RIGHTEOUSNESS

Much of our perpetuation of the unknown or false self can be directly correlated to our perception of Christ's humanity.

I didn't know what to do with my humanity. Similarly, I

didn't know what to do with *Christ's* humanity. The doctrine of original sin was so central to how I reflected on my identity that the possibility of the doctrine of original righteousness was beyond my grasp. I had overidentified Christ with his divinity and downplayed his humanity. Thinking that spirituality related only to divinity, I missed out on what was actually quite spiritual about my humanity.

In John's first chapter we find some of the richest biblical material to help understand the incarnation of God. The book opens up with "In the beginning there was the Word: and the Word was in God's presence, and the Word was God. . . . And the Word became flesh and stayed for a little while among us" (John 1:1, 14a).

> The incarnation of Christ was a restoration of creation.

John 1:1 actually is an echo of Genesis 1:1, which also starts with the exact same phrase, "In the beginning." What are the implications of this echo? Why would John reference the creation narrative as he's introducing incarnational theology?

My understanding is that the incarnation of Christ was a restoration of creation. Genesis 1:27 reads, "Humankind was created as God's reflection: in the divine image God created them," and verse 31 concludes, "God looked at all of this creation, and proclaimed that this was good—*very good*" (emphasis mine). Of course, this statement was made before Adam and Eve left Eden. But still, humanity . . . *very good*?

Seriously?

I have had a hard time seeing *anything* very good in my humanity.

I think John was pointing us to a recovery of goodness in creation—humanity in its best and purest sense, before sin gummed things up. This is what Reinhold Niebuhr popularized as *original righteousness*—not just innocence but faithfulness in relationship to God. However, the experience of sin defiled our original righteousness and set us spinning out of control. The woundedness of our humanity needed redemption, and God's incarnation through Christ introduced a possibility of that redemption. When God became human, the goodness in humanity was restored in Christ.

And with the possibility of restoration came the hope for redemption.

Christ submitted to the sacrament of baptism (John 1:29–34) not just to locate his identify with the community of faith but also to recover original righteousness: "We must do this to completely fulfill God's justice," or "righteousness," as translated in many other versions (Matthew 3:15).

Immediately following Christ's baptism, we see him move toward community. The Gospel of John recounts the legitimate human need Christ experienced for relationships. Jesus, the source and essence of love, needed relationships. Andrew, Simon, Philip, and Nathanael (John 1:35–51) responded to this extension of love by becoming the first disciples. Love cannot objectify its recipient. Love centers the other, making the object of its love the subject, the focus. Love—one of the ways we understand God ("for God is love," 1 John 4:8)—became embodied in humanity and was incarnated in Christ.

> When God became human, the goodness in humanity was restored in Christ.

The rest of John continues to point to the humanity of Christ by illustrating things such as Jesus's affirmation of human celebration and appetites at the wedding in Cana (John 2:1–12);

the recognition of passion and anger as genuine human expressions when Christ made a whip and cleared the Temple in Jerusalem (John 2:13–17); and when Jesus faced the limitations of his humanity by experiencing fatigue and thirst, "weary from the journey" at a well in Samaria (John 4:1–26). Thirst in this early reference foreshadows the thirst Christ experienced as he suffered on the cross (John 19).

These glimpses of Christ's human embodiment are celebrations of his humanity, and they become graces to us—invitations to receive our own human limitations.

Understanding the humanity of Christ has helped me embrace my own humanity. Seeing Jesus validate needs, behaviors, and passions that don't *seem* divine is an invitation for me to grasp the implications of his incarnation. I've come to understand that spiritual doesn't only mean divine but in some ways becomes the hinge between what is human and divine—and sometimes it's expressed in very material things, including my humanity.

THE DANGERS OF THE UNKNOWN SELF

I haven't seen many episodes of *American Idol,* but those I have were painful to watch. Clearly some of the contestants auditioning have been lied to about their perceived talent. Listening to the lies of others helps us avoid telling ourselves the truth. Sure, watching the spectacle of people try out for *American Idol* can be funny, but it's also pitiful. But when you get the equivalent of an unaware community member, it's far from amusing.

Perhaps the most dangerous people in communities are those who don't know themselves and don't understand the need to awaken to their identity. I've served alongside quite a few people who misdiagnosed themselves on any one of the temperament tests we use. Some approached the personality assessment tools by testing for who they wanted to be, not who they were. In addition to arriving at inaccurate results, some of them then attempted to live into a version of someone they obviously weren't. Such scenarios end in disaster.

This happens a lot with people who want to lead but may not have the internal qualities to pull a group together or rally a team around a common purpose. I've seen quite a few folks who took leadership courses and read the best management books but still didn't have the presence and self-confidence to pull leadership off. When those folks inserted themselves into positions of influence, they failed. Miserably. And their failures impacted a lot of people around them.

The problem in not knowing ourselves is that lack of self-awareness can really hurt those around us. That's why we need people to be honest with us. Our friends need to help protect us from the public humiliation that seems to shock so many *American Idol* contestants.

I recently heard someone say that we are the average of the five people with whom we spend the most time. Pretty bad logic if taken to a circular conclusion of repetitive reshaping: it could get so insular and incestuous that you and your five closest friends would eventually morph into one version of your collective selves. But who we are does seem to be largely connected to those with whom we are in relationship.

Every time I get hit up by a Facebook friend request from someone I don't immediately recognize or don't know, even before I open her or his profile page, I click on the "mutual friends" link to see whom the person knows. Getting a sense of whom someone is connected to is often a more realistic snapshot of who the requester might be. At least it can be fairer than any polished digital identities that we create and put out for the world to see.

> Lack of self-awareness can really hurt those around us.

Our identities are never isolated realities. Fundamentally, I believe, we are defined by our relationships, and the strength of those relationships helps us grow into deeper levels of self-awareness.

IDENTITY CLAIMS THE GIFTS OF ITS COMMUNITY

Mukti, the former sex worker mentioned in a previous chapter, claimed the gift of her name, Freedom. As the members of her community, Sari Bari, moved deeper into commitments with one another, they began to look beyond their group and considered extending their freedom to young women who were vulnerable to trafficking. Since many of the women in Sari Bari had been trafficked themselves, they knew the profile of the young girls who would potentially be targeted. They knew the tricks of the traffickers. They knew the towns and villages frequently targeted by those who sold people into slavery. So the women of Sari Bari organized themselves around the vision of prevention units.

They launched their first prevention unit near the India-Bangladesh border. I've visited it a number of times. It's a place of peace with lots of natural light flooding in, illuminating the life and laughter of the place. The young women employed at the community center are taught to sew quilts, scarves, and purses, but they are also given the opportunity to learn to read and write, skills essential to combating the vulnerabilities of poverty. The women spend their mornings sewing gorgeous artisan products and their afternoons studying Bengali.

During one of my visits, I purchased a training blanket that a young woman was learning to stitch on. Just like the other women of Sari Bari, who sign their names to each blanket they produce, I found the tag on the training blanket I had bought. The tag read "Mukti," but I knew that wasn't the name of the young girl who had sewn that particular piece.

I inquired about the name and was told all the girls in the prevention unit sign their blankets "Mukti." *Freedom.* What a profound gift those girls received, even though none had ever been enslaved in the sex trade. Many of them would never know how to fully appreciate that freedom, but they laid claim to opportunity through the sacrifices of the formerly enslaved members of Sari Bari.

Our relationships affirm our identities. In community, then, we can claim the gift of identity ascribed by those around us. In community we can be free.

EMBRACING THE WHOLE OF WHO WE ARE

She was in fifth grade when she accidentally found her adoption papers. Through the eyes of a child, she read page after page, tears trickling down her cheeks. She discovered that, as a newborn, she'd been abandoned at a bus station in Shanghai, China. Someone had found her and taken her to a police station, which had turned her over to an orphanage where she was named Hua Ming Lei. An Irish-American couple living on the East Coast of the United States adopted her and brought her to their home, renaming her Margaret Cecilia O'Leary. At university she met Miguel, a Mexican American, who would become her husband. At their wedding she took his last name, Garcia. And so she has lived with Chinese, Irish, and Mexican names.

Margaret has come to terms with the gift of her identities, the gift of her names and heritages, but she rests in one name: Beloved. She claims her beloved-ness and allows it to offer understanding and support to those who struggle with abandonment and alienation. She does not let any of the versions of who she has been or who she is now to claim all of her: rather, she rests in the gifts each name has bestowed upon her. She is much more complex and beautiful than just one of her names alone. She refuses to let herself be reduced to any one of her identities. Her true identity transcends them all.

> Margaret has come to terms with the gift of her names and heritages, but she rests in one name: Beloved.

One of the greatest challenges in our journeys of discovery toward an awakened identity is the difficult task of resisting urges toward reductionism. As much as we can avoid over-identifying with the bad things we experience or our flaws, we simultaneously need to learn to avoid finding value in the good we accomplish. Even harder is learning to resist the comfort of overidentification with our life's most simple roles, functions, or ties.

Father Emmanuel Katongole is a Ugandan Catholic priest who cofounded Duke Divinity School's Center for Reconciliation. I consider him one of my most treasured friends. On several occasions he's spoken to me about the tendency of the fragments of his life to perceive themselves as the whole.

One such conversation happened after he presided over a Sunday Mass at a local parish near Chapel Hill, North Carolina. Though I'd known him for almost ten years, it was the first time I had seen him lead a liturgical service. After church we grabbed lunch and I commented on how impressed I had been with his homily, on how inviting and intimate Mass had seemed as he led the congregation in worship.

This was a new side of him, and I was trying to find a category and space for how I had understood his vocation. He told me how difficult it is for all the moving pieces of our world to have a full sense of who we are in the variety of ways we live our vocations.

He spoke of his bishop in Uganda, who had given him permission to teach at Duke Divinity School. To his bishop, he was first and foremost a priest in his local Ugandan diocese, but at Duke, he was a tenured professor who was expected to function as any other celebrated and accomplished Duke faculty member. Emmanuel had cofounded and subsequently became the codirector of the Center for Reconciliation and as a leader of that organization had shouldered many of the responsibilities of running that movement. These two roles sometimes came into conflict with each other. As a professor, Emmanuel was expected to teach, but the demands of the center often made finding time to lecture a near impossibility. In addition to all this, Emmanuel had helped start a small Catholic charity that was helping dig wells and provide clean drinking water in Uganda. He was expected to help lead that organization on top of all he was already giving himself to. Emmanuel is an author, having published several excellent books, each of them better than the one prior. Then, on Sundays, he serves a local parish as a priest, many of the congregants entirely unaware of the other significant parts of his life.

For most people, these would be way too many moving parts and far too many responsibilities, but Emmanuel is special and has a proper confidence in knowing who he is. It is in the groundedness of his core identity that he draws centeredness for vocational discovery, exploration, and commitments.

> From Emmanuel's freedom, we can see what it is to be free to live beautifully, faithfully, and unhindered by unrealistic expectations and external pressures.

Alexander Schmemann illustrated this in his personal journals: "The tragedy is that each fragment wants to be the whole— all of Orthodoxy—and passionately denies the others. . . . No one sees [her or his] limitations, [her or his] own relative character in Christ. I see my calling in trying—and praying—to overturn this approach, to unite all these fragments and to return them to life in and through Christ . . . because I understand these fragments and can identify literally with each of them."[2]

Emmanuel is one of those rare people who refuses to allow the fragments, all the bits and moving pieces of his life, to claim the whole of him. Rather, he allows the wholeness of his illuminated identity to shape how he lives faithfully into the various expressions of his core vocation.

Emmanuel is free. From his freedom, we can see what it is to be free to live beautifully, faithfully, and unhindered by unrealistic expectations and external pressures.

Margaret is free. She claims and lives into the truth of her belovedness, not allowing herself to overidentify who she is with the names she's been given.

Blanca is free. Her new name, Eliana, is an invitation for us to discover the new ways God allows us to re-create our futures by building off our pasts.

The young women in the Sari Bari prevention unit are free. In their freedom, we find a way forward to rediscover who we already are but have yet to claim.

We can be free. Resisting the urge toward reductionism and rejecting the lies that attempt to diminish our belovedness, we can discover who we are and allow it to be lived beautifully through us.

Betraying Community

Kissing One Another to Death

The person who comes into a fellowship because [he is] running away from [himself is] misusing it for the sake of diversion, no matter how spiritual this diversion may appear.
—Dietrich Bonhoeffer

If you stay in any relationship or community long enough, you will experience betrayal—not personal betrayal, though that certainly happens, but betrayal of community, of relationship.

That can happen when we betray ourselves by not living up to our own standards. Betrayals of community may be experienced as immature and selfish attempts at loving those around you. Perhaps it's as naive as merely unintentionally manipulating the vulnerabilities in our friendships. However it happens, all of us betray our communities and friendships, and all of us are betrayed by them. It's part of the metanarrative of all great human stories. Betrayal is one of the perplexing and peculiar gifts that comes from weaving our lives together with others. And our response to betrayal can be a powerful force, setting our life trajectories toward grace or bitterness.

How you experience and respond to betrayals in relationships ultimately impacts who you—and your community—become.

THIRTY SILVER COINS:
THE COST OF NOT LOVING WELL

Judas, one of the disciples of Christ, committed one of the most memorable betrayals of relationship in history. In the gospel of Matthew, chapter 26:14–16, Judas negotiates a price, thirty pieces of silver, to turn Christ over for trial. The placement of this passage of Scripture is interesting. Earlier in the same chapter, we are given one of the Bible's most tender and moving stories. In it, a woman pours an exquisite bottle of precious perfume over Jesus in what must have been one of the all-time most beautiful acts of adoration. In other readings of this story, Judas makes a statement of the obvious: that the cost of that perfume could have fed quite a few hungry people. It is a sensible and compassionate sentiment, but rather than being affirmed for this intervention toward justice, Judas is scolded by Christ in front of the other disciples for being too pragmatic.

Judas's concern for those who are poor must have been at the forefront of his mind because the passage immediately preceding this story commands us to care for those in need. The last fifteen verses in the twenty-fifth chapter of Matthew's Gospel end with Christ reflecting on a metaphor of judgment. He is separating humanity in terms of their response to poverty and human need. Those who were available to the hungry or sick were welcomed,

while those who failed to help the naked and
the imprisoned were sent away to be punished.

> **Judas committed one of the most memorable betrayals of relationship in history.**

Notice the significant nuance in this passage. Those rewarded for their righteousness
reply, "When?" They seem surprised. "When
did we see you hungry and feed you, or see
you thirsty and give you drink? When did we
see you as a stranger and invite you in, or clothe you in your
nakedness?" (vs. 37–38). They didn't know what they had done.
Apparently responding to need just came naturally to them.
Kindness and compassion were simply the obvious things to
do. So the righteous were surprised at being rewarded for being
themselves.

The unrighteous, however, respond with a bit of defensive-
ness: "When did we see you hungry or thirsty, or homeless or
naked, or ill or in prison, and not take care of you?" (vs. 44).
That little word, *not,* should jump out at us. It's the only difference between questions from the righteous and the unrighteous.
"When did I help?" versus "When did I *not* help?"

When did I help you? Are we surprised when we're thanked
for something that comes naturally, something we can't help but
want to do? Or, *When did I* not *help you?* Tucking that little
not into the response seems an attempt to justify themselves by
what they thought they *had done* rather than who they should
have *been.*

Looking at the story line, Jesus appears to be sending a mixed
message. What must Judas have thought? After all, Matthew
25:31–46 basically suggests that the fate of our souls hangs on
our response to human need. Immediately following this, Mat-

thew 26:1–13 tells a story of extravagant waste in light of a world in need. In fact, in the gospel of John, we're told that the cost of the perfume was a full year's wages.

Judas's head must have been spinning. Being scolded in front of his friends must have embarrassed him. He might have been frustrated and confused by the seemingly mixed messages Christ gave on responding to poverty. So off he goes . . .

To literally sell out his master.

Plenty of other backstories are at play here. Most Bible scholars suggest that as a radicalized political subversive, Judas wanted to force Christ's hand, to spark the long-awaited revolution many Jews longed for. Rather than suggesting that Judas betrayed Christ out of humiliation or frustration, most scholars give him the benefit of the doubt and claim he was trying to nudge along what appeared to be a reluctant messiah—a generous scrub on Judas's motivation for betrayal, one that softens the possible maliciousness of selling out a friend.

What might be the most surprising part of the story, though, is how the betrayal goes down. When first-century versions of rent-a-cops show up to arrest Jesus, they know he's their target. How?

By the signal of a kiss.
A kiss from Judas, a friend, is the sign of the betrayal.
Shocking.

There's a lot to reflect on here. If a relationship with Christ was betrayed (and no one ever extended love better than he did), it's little surprise that, in our flawed attempts to love one another, we might experience betrayal of our friendships or community too.

Nearly every time I talk about this with friends, it's as if I've unscrewed the handle of a faucet. Stories of heartache and betrayal pour out. Stories of betrayals in marriages or between family members. Stories of betrayals in companies, churches, and organizations. Stories of betrayal between lifelong friends. Just about everyone has a story of being or feeling betrayed.

> If a relationship with **Christ** was betrayed, it's little surprise that we might experience betrayal too.

Yet some of those events may not have been true betrayal—not in the worst sense of the word—because betrayal may not have been the intent. And because betrayal isn't just something that happens between us and others. Sometimes it's far more personal than that.

BETRAYAL OF SELF

Have you ever betrayed yourself? Have you ever done something that you never thought you'd do? Have you ever crossed a line that you wish you had never crossed? Have you ever compromised any of your dearest values or deepest convictions? Probably all of us have had to take a long, hard look in the mirror and admit to ourselves that we wish we'd done something different. Often, the disappointment we feel with ourselves comes from a form of personal betrayal—to values, convictions, morality, or our own sense of right and wrong.

When we betray ourselves, the consequences are almost never isolated, because those betrayals hurt those closest to us. Not being the best version of yourself means you have less to give in your relationships. So another shade on the color wheel of betrayal bleeds into our friendships and communities when we're not living into our own values, convictions, morality, or sense of right and wrong. How many of us have heard, "You really let me down" or "Your actions betrayed who I thought you were"?

Sure, it's not fair to put unrealistic expectations on anyone, ourselves included, but sometimes those around us experience our personal failures as betrayals.

This can create a nasty little cycle of betrayal. So you messed up, betrayed yourself. Now you have to put the pieces back together, and as a result, someone who needed more from you or looked up to you feels betrayed by your failure. People's responses usually don't help. In fact, it may aggravate a bad situation. When you most need support, companionship, or friendship, the people you look to for those things feel betrayed by your mistake. And when that happens, you may start to experience their disappointment as a form of betrayal against your friendship.

> Everyone gets lost in the tragic cycle of self-betrayal and mismanaged expectations.

And on it goes, round and round.

Everyone gets lost in the tragic cycle of self-betrayal and mismanaged expectations. Misunderstandings fuel the pain-filled circle. Blame heightens the justification for one's feelings of disappointment and betrayal. Somehow, though, in these sorts of experiences, everyone feels she or he is the victim rather than the perpetrator of betrayal.

BETRAYAL AS AN IMMATURE
ATTEMPT TO LOVE

Many of the times when we fail our communities and those failures are experienced as betrayals, it's safe to say that we don't realize what we're doing. Some of us have a hard time naming and understanding basic things such as our own needs and so act out in ways that hurt others. Some of us have never been loved the way we needed to be and subconsciously carry our wounds into our relationships by not knowing how to love others well. Some of us live in tremendous fear and keep intimacy at arm's length. Though we attempt to love, the inadequacy of our ability to do so well is often experienced by others as a form of betrayal.

It's important to note that in authentic relationships and dynamic communities, most betrayals are simply immature expressions of love. In nearly every instance of betrayal I've experienced in community, if I can take a step or two back and objectively reflect on the situation, I'd have to say that the feeling of being betrayed was a legitimate experience, but the *cause* of the betrayal—and the ensuing feelings—was often a misunderstanding.

Accepting someone in failure is actually pretty tough, and loving that person by extending grace is even tougher. Have you ever had a friend pull back in a relationship "for your own good"? Many people experience that as betrayal.

Perhaps you've struggled with an addiction or been in a codependent relationship, or maybe you've walked away from your faith or transitioned out of a community.

During those vulnerable, fragile times, it's unlikely that you were the best version of yourself. I'm betting that the same thing that happens to me happens to you—that during some of the hardest times of your life you haven't been the best friend you could be.

It may be that, when that happened, you found yourself on the receiving end of what people call "tough love." Yes, there are times when true tough love is necessary. In the face of a devastating addiction, it may even be the only option. But the phrase "tough love" has also become something people like to use when they think they're taking the moral high ground. Too often the reality isn't that it's the only option left but rather that it's hard to love someone who is in a hard place. When love becomes inconvenient, those folks walk away.

> When love
> becomes
> inconvenient,
> some folks walk
> away.

Sadly, in this situation, so-called tough love lacks any real love and usually directs more love at our value systems than at the other person. This kind of "tough love" is about punishment rather than discipline, preventing acceptance and grace.

Even so, we need to realize that when someone stops calling or abandons the friendship "for your own good," what she or he is probably doing is creating some much-needed space to catch his or her breath, get a different perspective on things, take a break from a difficult relationship, or try to communicate disapproval with how you're living or acting. Generally the intentions are benevolent, but the language is a bit off. Usually "for your own good" is really for the good of the person saying it. Maybe that's why we experience these kinds of separations as betrayals. They can be confusing. And too often they come at the worst times.

We can feel betrayed by a kiss in numerous ways. Ultimately,

the notion of betrayal by a kiss implies intimacy and connect-
edness. We typically don't kiss those we aren't close to, and a
complete stranger typically doesn't betray us.

That is why betrayal hurts so much. That is why betrayal gets
so messy.

RESPONDING TO THE INEVITABLE: LOVE

Sometimes I think the true betrayals in life are fewer than we
realize. Sure, sometimes friends with malicious intentions really
do sell us out. But most betrayals are misguided attempts at love
or painfully tragic comedies of errors. I want to be clear that
most of what seems to be betrayal in relationships is simply
ways of loving each other poorly. This is reinforced by the reality that you really can't be betrayed outside of a relationship.

Betrayals of community are, to a large extent, letdowns caused
by unfulfilled expectations. Expectations imply an exchange of
some sort and point to spoken or unspoken bonds that hold
people together. Expectations weave our lives together, so when
we fail to meet them, it's as if we're pulling at the seams of our
relationships.

There's a valuable lesson to learn in the friendship between
Judas and Jesus: the betrayal by Judas in response to the love
of Christ isn't the metric of success in their relationship. Rather,
Christ's fidelity in loving Judas *in the midst of betrayal* is the sign
of faithfulness and the standard to follow.

I can't find any instances when Christ pulled back in relationship from anyone for that person's "own good." Somehow
though, many Christians have a very flawed understanding of

love in relationships. What does love look like in light of disappointment, failure, and betrayal?

Is it possible to shake free from the entanglement of expectations (fair or otherwise), the hurt of disappointments, or the need for boundaries in our relationships without betrayal? Can we negotiate these layers of relationships without forcing blame? How can we name the limitations of our relationships without using them (even unintentionally) as a weapon to hurt others?

We will experience betrayal in communities, relationships, and friendships. Our feelings of being betrayed are legitimate, and the pain is real. However, let us learn from the example of Christ and find a way to extend love and seek to understand how the flawed motivations of those who love us can also hurt us. In finding the eyes to see the causes of our betrayals, we may end up finding better ways to love those who've betrayed us.

FRIENDSHIP: THE BASIS FOR COMMUNITY

In community, friendship is sometimes missed entirely. It's ironic that people will come together to form community for the sake of community. It's a curiosity when I observe groups of people struggling to form community, when they first and foremost aren't even friends.

Fundamentally, friendship is the basis of community. If we don't have the gift of friendship in weaving our lives together, our communities are simply experimental spaces set up to fail or to lead to deep resentments.

This often catches us off guard, but truthfully, community

can expose people's inability to be true friends. I think back on how many friendships have been ruined in community simply because our notions of community got in the way of forming friendships.

The Franciscan mystic Father Richard Rohr talks about this in his teaching on community. Speaking from nearly fifty years in community, Rohr reflects on the danger of those who join communities for the sake of community, apart from real relationships *within* community. He describes such folks as people arriving with a script and everyone else in the community as playing a role—a role that they're bound to fail in because they don't know they're being used. People with a script have predetermined how the community will be used, they've already mentally narrated how community will meet their own needs, and they idealize notions of community apart from the reality of what communities are made up of: real, flawed, and broken people.

> Fundamentally, friendship is the basis of community.

Donald Nicholl also wrote about this after spending four years as rector of the Ecumenical Institute at Tantur, near Jerusalem, where he worked to develop a theologically grounded Christian response to the ongoing conflict in the Holy Land. In his journal he wrote about those who love their notions of community at the expense of the people or friendships involved in community: "That heavy matter is now blocking the flow of life and love within the community; and the worst of it is that it is precisely those who talk most about community-building who block the flow, because they are carrying around with them, like a lead ball attached to their waists . . . that whenever someone came along full of talk about the need to 'build community,' then

[one] could be pretty sure that such a person would prove disruptive of whatever community (not ideal but real) had already been established."[1]

In the original version of his journals he also wrote about those who would look beyond individuals, through friendships, to control communities: "In this community as in many others, there are the sort who often make the running, set the tone or fix the agenda, whatever metaphor you wish to use. I had already come across Bonhoeffer's remark, that if someone arrives upon the scene talking perpetually about community then you can be more or less certain that they will turn out to be a pain in the neck of the existing community onto which they have descended. What such characters usually mean is that they have devised a scenario for the community in which the rest of us play supporting roles to themselves who are to star as the central character in the drama. A community can carry only one or two people like that, but if you get more than a certain percentage of such prima donnas the tension of the drama becomes intolerable for the other members."[2]

Without authentic relationships, community is merely a backdrop for someone's journey of self-discovery, and community members are used up along the way.

FRIENDSHIP AS A REMEDY FOR BETRAYAL

In 1995 I shared a flat in South India with a couple of friends from college. That year we made frequent trips up to Kolkata to do volunteer work with Mother Teresa and the Missionaries of Charity. One rainy night we took refuge in a restaurant for dinner. Since we ordered too much food, we packed our left-overs to go. After leaving the little hole in the wall, we walked down a side alley and bumped into a quiet, unassuming home-less man with big pleading eyes. Trying to stay dry, he was sitting on the side of the road wrapped in a blanket. Though he didn't ask, we offered him what remained of our dinner, and he gladly accepted.

That's my first memory of Tuna. Since meeting him, I have never been the same. Tuna has become a sort of proxy commu-nity member for us.

Tuna sleeps on the sidewalk across the street from one of Kolkata's largest outdoor markets. He spends his days outside the Government Art College. Tuna carries all he owns in a bag or tied up in a blanket. He usually has some old notebooks or a newspaper completely filled with sketches and drawings scratched down with a blue ink ballpoint pen. Sometimes he has an extra shirt or a tiny bar of soap; every once in a while he even manages to find a toothbrush for his few remaining teeth, but that's about all. Occasionally he makes friends with a street dog (or a pack of mangy dogs) that follows him around and sleeps with him at night on the sidewalk. A mere ninety-six pounds, Tuna looks as though he could be twenty years older than he actually is.

> Since meeting Tuna, I have never been the same.

If you saw him on the street, you might give him some change, but most of us wouldn't give him the time of day. Tuna is a visibly broken man. Sadness is carved into his face. His kind eyes reflect a deep sense of the tragic.

Though we first bumped into him back in 1995, it wasn't until a few years later that I got to know him. Over time, many of our community members have worked to cultivate a friendship with Tuna. Getting to know him hasn't been easy. For the most part, Tuna lives in his own world, and trying to tap into his mind is as difficult a task as any. When someone *is* able to make a tangible connection with him, it's short-lived and easily interrupted by the slightest of distractions.

People who live and work in the area where Tuna spends most of his time have filled in some of the mysterious gaps about his past. They say that he was a talented and successful art student until something terrible happened to his brother (another version of the story hints at a lost love). Whatever that crisis was, something so traumatic happened that it broke Tuna under its burden, forcing him to the streets. He has never been the same since, and it seems unlikely that he will ever be the same again.

> **Tuna is looking for an opportunity to be known and accepted.**

Most of our interactions with Tuna happen over a meal at Khalsa's, a little Northwestern Frontier restaurant run by a kind Punjabi Sikh family. Over the years, a number of us have contributed to a running tab or account, allowing Tuna to eat a couple meals a day there—for most of us not a big deal, but for a homeless man an answer to his prayers.

But Tuna doesn't like to eat alone. So, sadly, he often goes without meals while he waits on the streets, looking for a friend to join him for lunch. Though he expects you to pay for it, he is not looking for a handout. He is looking for an opportunity to be known and accepted over a near-boiling cup of sweet milky tea (with lots and lots of sugar) or a plate of fish curry.

When he sees a friend, he shouts out her or his name and comes running. He immediately asks to be taken to lunch or at least for a cup of tea. He also loves to see movies if someone will take him—especially if they have "good action." But a movie is never enough; ice cream is always in order once the movie is over.

Over many meals we've sat with Tuna and tried to get him to talk about himself. After gentle persistence, he sometimes begins to recall things from his "old life." In eruptions of surprising vulnerability, he has said that he had three brothers and sisters. He's said that his real name is Dipankar Pal (a typical Bengali name). He seems to want to remember, but something won't let him.

An artist, Tuna is constantly drawing. And as a form of payment for the meals provided on his behalf, he loves to draw the faces of the friends with whom he eats. Nearly every one of those precious portraits is scribbled out on a slightly used Khalsa's napkin. As he sits down with a pen and begins to fill whatever paper he has at hand with tiny, seemingly confusing little scratches and lines—that magically become the portrait of whomever he is sitting with—he shares his story bit by bit.

Inspired by one of these meals, Matt Ammerman wrote a moving song about friendship with Tuna, "Don't Let Me Eat Alone":

He put his paintbrushes away for a few
The masterpiece become a fool
He likes painting people he will never know
They are high and he is low

He draws my portrait and through confusing lines
I see my face yeah it is mine

I go to bed; the subject is for me so light
But for you it's very, very cold tonight

I like crows man and I read Edgar Allen Poe
'Cause he's a poet don't you know
He took it fast, let's take it slow
And he said
I never read any of Poe
So he's a poet, I guess you'd know
I don't think so good and I speak kinda slow

I never did read that much, but man I'd like a bite of
   lunch
Don't make me eat alone
Do I ask of you too much?

I guess I could put down my book for a while
Just to enjoy your crooked smile
The pages don't give me the same sort of effect
'Cause I like your face and your dialect

And I want to know just who you are
But your words evade like covered stars
You don't deserve this life you live
To be the joke of some street kid
If I met this devil in your head
I'd push him down till he was dead

It's a tragedy and it's killing me
This daily mental killing spree

Hey, if I could help you
I'd really love to
Yeah if I could help you
I'd really love to

I never read any of Poe
So he's a poet I guess you'd know
But I don't think so good and I speak kinda slow
I never did read that much, but man I'd like a bite of
    lunch
Don't let me eat alone
Do I ask of you too much?[3]

Tuna's napkin sketches speak truth. A good friend who also happens to be an artist commented after observing Tuna's drawings, "I appreciate the vitality and the magic of drawing. In a few lines with a ballpoint pen on a napkin, a human person appears. It is a record of an intimate dinner conversation. The pen is the sensitive instrument able to carry a pulse and the tender humanity of the person holding it."

Another friend reflected on his own portrait, which Tuna had drawn, "A friend recently penned a picture of me on a napkin as we shared lunch together. What he created conjured up many of these thoughts in a moment of hopefulness. His crooked lines and scribbles provided a portrait that depicted much more than myself. It helped me to see, with new eyes, the humanity that has been gifted to us."

The napkins we walk away with are a tangible reminder that, although Tuna is in fact quite poor and those of us who have entered Tuna's circle of friends have vocationally come to serve Jesus among those in poverty, we receive so much from him. Most especially an invitation to be known and accepted.

Now, if I'm honest, it's sometimes a stretch to call my relationship with Tuna a friendship. To most outside observers, it would appear that I receive very little in our exchanges. We have almost nothing in common except a handful of shared friends. It usually feels as though Tuna only takes from me and asks me for things. But if I didn't allow for this relationship to press me into a discovery of love, I would be betraying him by using his vulnerabilities to bolster myself. He has needs, and I can meet some of them.

Folks like Tuna become targets for good-hearted and concerned people. Whether unconsciously or intentionally, we exploit guys like him by taking advantage of their poverty for either our personal formation and discipleship or to make ourselves feel good. These forms of betrayal are manipulative and dehumanize everyone involved.

> We receive so much from Tuna. Most especially an invitation to be known and accepted.

Being friends with Tuna has been transformational for our entire community. It has challenged us to move from a mentality of programmed ministry to one of relationship.

For so long, many of us have perpetuated a mentality that has been one of ministering to people who are poor as objects and passive recipients of compassion and charity. But Tuna has reminded us of our need to include those who are poor in our lives through intimate relationships—not to see those trapped in poverty as people we "minister to," but as people with whom we identify.

Being in a relationship with Tuna has allowed us to move from donor to receptor.

When we view him as a person with an intrinsic dignity that points to his proper identity, we receive tremendous gifts from him. In our efforts and prayers to help "liberate" Tuna from his physical, emotional, and spiritual poverty, we have found ourselves being liberated by his presence in the life of our community.

Though we had hoped to give to Tuna, he always seems to give us more.

Friendship with Tuna teaches us new insights regarding the need to learn to love better. As hard as getting to Tuna might be, it's easy to love him. People with special needs, those who are vulnerable and pushed to the margins, open up tender areas of our hearts that invite love to dismantle selfish notions of relationship.

This scrub on expectations helps illuminate the ways in which we love one another poorly—and the ways in which misappropriated love can lead to betrayal.

Tuna's story is unfinished. It's a restless reminder of process and longing. Though he's been offered all forms of assistance, he opts to stay on the streets and live on his own terms. As strange as this might sound to others, he has his rhythm of life.

> We are continually the rough draft of an unfinished novel.

Though we know that we are continually the rough draft of an unfinished novel, what's unresolved in Tuna's life is painful both for him and for many of his friends. The stories of our lives will perpetually be unfinished and unresolved. In our relationship with Tuna, we are reminded that when we befriend people who are poor, our job is not to save them—a benevolent form of betrayal—but to join together on a journey of love.

This is one of the challenges of being in a friendship with Tuna. But it is those who seemingly have nothing to give who will give us the most. In seeking to love God, we must follow

God's children—those who are weak or vulnerable—with an expression of that love embodied through voices reminding us to keep our love pure.

Because our notions of friendship can be narrow and limiting, Tuna has become my guide, forcing me to rethink what friendship is. Sure, being with Tuna is difficult and can be extremely demanding, but it's in these kinds of relationships that we are best able to explore the mysteries of receiving through the gift of giving.

You see, most of our friendships can be incredibly self-serving or self-affirming. Typically we surround ourselves with friends who reflect back to us a mirror of our self, the false center that is perpetuated by the kinds of circles we insulate ourselves in. Friendships are one of life's greatest gifts, but they take real work and require quite a bit of effort if we want them to be authentic.

What I love about my friendship with Tuna is that it isn't based on what he offers me but what emerges between us when we're together. We both become someone greater than ourselves when we're able to share time, space, and life. And when we're not together, I attempt to live a life that reflects respect for the way that he suffers, hoping that I continue to be a good friend to him while we're apart.

Tuna's acceptance of me isn't based on the good or bad things I've done. I'm pretty sure he doesn't really care much about my achievements and disappointments. Tuna wants to be accepted, known, and loved.

True friends are the people in your life who aren't surprised by your accomplishments or disappointed by your tragic failures. Your true

> **True friends are the people in your life who aren't surprised by your accomplishments or disappointed by your tragic failures.**

friends know you enough to manage their expectations around the sense that we're not as bad as our worst moments and often worse than our best.

Discovering new kinds of friendships—that dismantle our unfair expectations and take the focus off of ourselves—helps ground our other relationships. And learning to love each other well, accepting the best and worst of each other, focusing on our relationships as they are rather than what we think they should be, helps us stay faithful to our friendships, relationships, and communities.

Incompatibility

When Together Is Too Close

> Community is a place of conflict; conflict inside each one of
> us. There is first of all the conflict between the values of the
> world and the values of community, between togetherness
> and independence.
>
> —Jean Vanier

Chemistry is one of those elusive intangibles that every community needs to learn to manage. What should we do when members of our community seem completely incompatible? Or, on the flip side, what happens when the energy between people is so positive that it makes maintaining boundaries hard and leads to inappropriate friendships or relationships? How can we manage members in our community who might have a little bit too much chemistry—especially when it leads to attraction between people who are already married to others or in committed relationships?

Negotiating the gifts that emerge when chemistry is present or absent requires a good bit of self-awareness, critical reflection, and basic maturity.

It's just commonsense sort of stuff. Plain and simple. But sometimes, as they say, common sense is far from common.

THE GIFT OF CHEMISTRY

Chemistry is one of those things that tend to surprise us. When we're actively looking for effortless connections, we almost never find them. And the more we yearn for natural compatibility, the more painful the absence of chemistry in our present relationships can be. We all want to be understood by friends who just seem to "get us," without our having to explain. A lot of us are worn out from trying to make friendships work with friends who would seem to be perfect matches in our social settings but who, in reality, aren't. Often, rather than being ramped up with energy from time spent with those we're closest to, many of us feel worn out after being with them.

When you have chemistry in your relationships, there's a palpable difference—something you can't explain, something that can't be forced, and something that can't be externally manufactured. Chemistry is a gift.

CHEMISTRY AND MATURITY

Sadly, over the past several years, the simmering crisis of immaturity and the subsequent male social disengagement have only grown more pronounced.

And our communities have paid a heavy price because of it.

There's been a statistical surge in North America in the numbers of women participating in nearly every cultural domain of social practice. More women than men are enrolling in universities. On top of that, once enrolled, the dropout rate is higher among men, while graduating classes consist of more and more female students.

A recent population survey noted that more men under the age of thirty (both as a percentage and in absolute numbers) are currently living at home with their parents than before World War II. This crisis of male adultolescence illustrates the lack of male social engagement and maturity. All of which leads to the one question:

Where are the men?

> Negotiating the gifts that emerge when chemistry is present or absent requires a good bit of self-awareness, critical reflection, and basic maturity.

The gender disparity in religious communities is even more pronounced. Christianity is demographically a worshipping community of women led by men. If you're a Christian woman committed to marrying a man who shares your religious convictions and principles, you may be forced into a form of social celibacy simply because in communities of faith women significantly outnumber men.

I've witnessed this trend firsthand. When Phileena and I began leading our community in 1996, our early relaunch team consisted of five single guys and a young married couple. Over the course of nearly twenty years, a community that was made up largely of young, single men became an organization in which women hold 75 percent of the international leadership positions. During a typical application review cycle, it isn't uncommon for us to get thirty internship applications—and only three or four of them from males.

In addition to men's lack of socialized maturity, vocations marked by compassionate service may be more culturally acceptable careers for women than for men. The externalized social pressure for men to provide, lead, or gain power is countercultural to the ethos of our community, one where powerlessness is celebrated as a posture of humility and friendship.

Father Richard Rohr has done quite a bit of profound work on the journey of men into adulthood. He has conducted retreats and written books around the need for masculine awakening. His suggestions stand in clear contrast to the Promise Keepers' pep-rally model of chest pounding, attempts at gender role reductionism perpetuated in books such as *Wild at Heart,* or the versions of theological gender violence taught by many of the emerging neoreformers.

Rohr has examined many of the traditional male initiation ceremonies that adolescent boys experience on their way to adulthood. In most parts of the world, with the exception of the so-called Developed World, these rites of passage are crucial to the growing-up process for boys. Rohr notes that in almost every one of those ceremonies, blood is central to the passage. He comments that through menstruation, childbirth, and menopause, women routinely see their own blood and subsequently have a sense of coming to terms with their limitations. Those experiences are natural parts of a woman's biological rhythms, reminding them that they are alive. But when men see their own blood, they're afraid they're dying. For boys to mature into adulthood, they need to come to terms with their weakness and limitations, accepting them as gifts.

> For boys to mature into adulthood, they need to come to terms with their weakness and limitations, accepting them as gifts.

A healthy community creates space in which young men can release their potential access to power and find safe spaces to rest in their weakness and limitations.

Many of us haven't made this difficult journey without a lot of resistance.

We are thrilled to have so many women leading our community, being vocationally faithful to their callings. These women also create the much-needed intentional conflict to subvert patriarchal systems that have relegated to women only demeaning roles, to the diminishment of feminine participation (and subsequently masculine identity, as well). We celebrate women in leadership positions for all the rich and dynamic gifts they offer our collective consciousness and how they've led in fresh and imaginative ways.

But we simultaneously lament the lack of male engagement, participation, and maturity in community. This disproportionate participation of men and women leaves communities off kilter. The lack of male engagement in communities and relationships creates huge imbalances in what need to be the natural dynamics of groups coming together, growing together, and pressing each other on to maturity.

The disparate male-female participation has also aggravated some difficult strains in relationships where natural chemistry exists and where men find themselves being led by women. This is something that has proven difficult for a few of our men, whose social culturalization leads them to expect men to be in the leadership positions that many of our women hold.

A few years ago, I happened to be out of town during a weekly community prayer time. Eight or nine people, all of them women, showed up for prayer that morning. A few of the women got together after the meeting and discussed the grief in not having a balanced and diverse community to gather with, not being able to blend and weave together the voices and prayers of men *and* women opening their souls together before God.

Subsequently, a season of lament unfolded in our community, grieving for the imbalance and holes created in not having the full gender participation of men and women working, serving, and worshipping together.

One of the things that's problematic about all this is the inability of some men to engage in community. To a certain extent, this is an issue of social maturity. Of course, maturity isn't the only factor involved here, and I realize that the factors perpetuating male withdrawal are complex. The reasons have been debated and will continue to undergo intense scrutiny, but for the time being we are treading water in religious communities largely made up of women but still led by men. There's no denying that this creates quite a few problems, especially when it comes to curating communal chemistry.

One such problem occurs when men and women who share a natural, effortless chemistry forge deep friendships or intense working relationships. Without the parameters of maturity to guide how these relationships are nurtured, affairs or sexual misconduct seem to sneak up on people. Rather than recognizing the sometimes awkward but obvious attraction between people, they usually pull back from the potential of cultivating relationships—both friendships and working partnerships—with someone to whom they're attracted.

But when accountable and transparent boundaries go overlooked, when communities (especially those made up largely of women but led by men) play to the potential weaknesses, vulnerabilities, or immaturities of men in these kinds of relationships, they end up further limiting the participation of women—and this is simply another form of misogyny or patriarchy.

THE UNEXPECTED GIFT OF
TOO MUCH CHEMISTRY

What happens in intense working relationships, friendships, or community settings when connections seem effortless and natural?

I spent part of the morning of my wedding day running the typical last-minute errands that always seem to sidetrack a soon-to-be groom. One of them happened to be driving a member of my wedding party to pick up his tuxedo. He was one of my first friends to get married, so I was trying to score some veteran advice from him as to what I could expect during my first year of marriage.

Without pause he promptly offered one of the most surprising bits of counsel I received that week: "Negotiating your friendships with women you're attracted to is one of the hardest parts of marriage."

Whaaaaaat?

I was taken back and offended that he would imply the mere possibility that I'd find anyone other than Phileena attractive. Even worse, suggesting such a thing just hours before I made my vows to her seemed audacious and insensitive.

Of course, that such attractions happen isn't news to anyone who's been married or in a committed relationship. Attraction is one of the beautiful things that makes us human. It's complex, complicated, and almost always out of our control.

Often similarities, shared interests, compatible personalities and temperaments, or common callings draw people together. At the beginning

> "Negotiating your friendships with women you're attracted to is one of the hardest parts of marriage."

of these newly formed communities and friendships there's often a high level of enthusiasm and energy. It's easy to "crush" on new friendships, throwing a lot of ourselves into the possibilities of what the relationships could become. It can be euphoric.

But what happens when the excitement wears off? Or when the energy around new friendships turns to attraction?

Most of the crushes people experience in friendships aren't sexual, but the connections can lead to deep intimacy, both emotional and sexual. When attractional impulses collide with effortless, natural chemistry, friendships generally play out in one of several ways. Mostly we hear about how they end badly for everyone. Rarely do we find the courage to recognize them, navigate them with maturity and honesty, and allow them to strengthen the bonds of all our existing relationships. Part of the problem is that many of us have never been trained to handle an unexpected attraction we experience toward someone other than our partner.

One of history's most underexamined yet clearly visible stories of charged chemistry has to be the relationship between St. Francis and St. Clare of Assisi. It's obvious that they shared some degree of natural compatibility, but their response to compatibility fueled them toward something greater than themselves. It goes without saying that there would have been no St. Clare without the catalytic example of St. Francis, and Francis would never have become who he was without the support and prayers of Clare forging a way for him and

> Sometimes using ultracharged chemistry by making space between two people generates more creativity, activity, and impact.

carrying his legacy forward after he was gone. Sometimes using ultracharged chemistry by making space between two people generates more creativity, activity, and impact. Learning to use natural affinity and compatibility can lead to great fecundity.

NEGOTIATING CHEMISTRY AND ATTRACTION

It's not fair to say I was a victim of my religious socialization, but I would say I felt a good bit stifled in the church and Christian university that incubated my passage to adulthood. Within a heterosexist environment, the instruction given to me and my peers suggested that members of the opposite sex should never work alone together behind closed doors and should never travel alone together or even share a meal without one of their partners present.

This seemed to be sensible advice for anyone for whom chemistry and attraction may be an issue, but it implied that adults couldn't control themselves. It also disqualified the possibility that navigating attraction and chemistry was a gift in and of itself. Rather than teaching self-awareness, I, as a man attracted to women, was taught to avoid the potential of working with women—specifically, though never explicitly stated, attractive women around my age group.

This was not so subtly modeled in many of the religious communities I participated in. Almost without exception, the secretaries that pastors or other religious professionals hired were older, and either they were expected to exhibit a certain sense of primness and distance or they were perceived to lack any sort of visible dynamic sexual energy.

Maybe these practices and policies have been fortified because, in many cases, people don't know how to handle the attractional forces of chemistry. In such failures communities are torn apart, friendships are devastated, and committed relationships are betrayed.

Without maturity, a healthy sense of boundaries, and a disciplined sense of self-control, setting policies may well be necessary. But we can be better, and we can do better. We can name effortless chemistry as a gift in community, and we can learn to handle it in honoring ways. Otherwise, we dishonor one another by reducing one another to potential threats—placing the blame on the threat rather than owning up to our vulnerabilities.

REEXAMINING AVOIDANCE AND REDUCTIONISM

As mentioned at the beginning of this chapter, I have found myself surrounded by a community that is increasingly made up of more and more women. And, truth be told, many of my fellow community members have been and are very attractive.

It would be misleading to suggest that I've been able to balance chemistry and attraction without a few bumps along the way. When I've not handled these tensions well, not surprisingly it's created some detrimental fallout in community, painful loss of friendships, and strains in my marriage. Reflecting back on some of the fallout, I've learned that self-awareness needs to be clearly present and nurtured in the safety of an understanding community or in the context of trusted, private spiritual direction or mentoring relationships.

First, we have to affirm the reality and inevitability that there will be someone in our circle of friends or community to whom we are or will eventually be attracted. For some of us, this might feel like an uncomfortable confession, but making it an observation untangles any sense of fear associated with this possibility. We are human; attractions will happen. It's that simple.

> **We are human; attractions will happen. It's that simple.**

I'm concerned about people who aren't able to be honest with themselves about this. When we're not candid regarding such things or when we try to push these urges deep within ourselves to deny or avoid them, they end up sanding down part of the dynamic nature of our humanity. Even worse, like trying to hold a beach ball under water, the further down we push these things, the higher they come flying up when we finally do lose control.

Given the inevitability of attraction, the worn-out, thin advice of avoidance must be reexamined. Though appearing to be sensible, it's unrealistic to live a life that's so insulated and isolated that we never find ourselves behind a closed door with someone of the opposite sex or with someone to whom we're attracted. Many of our current interactions with others are marked by "behind-the-door" exchanges already—such as meeting with our doctors, professors, accountants, or bosses. For the most part, we handle these social and professional relationships with maturity. Transferring this maturity—and discovering unexpected gifts in our other relationships—is a simple practice of social consistency.

Second, rather than being uncomfortable or fearful of natural attraction, we need to be able to recognize it as a gift in our relationships. Recognizing effortless chemistry between people can allow us to harness the creative energy toward our own personal wholeness. Unfortunately, what typically happens is that we overreact when attraction seems to sneak up on us in our community or relationships. The ensuing knee-jerk correction can lead to establishing boundaries that are intended to protect ourselves but sometimes end up by limiting all of our relationships. The challenge is not to legislate the boundaries of all our relationships based on our most vulnerable ones but to take each relationship for what it is and find the gifts therein.

Third, maybe our growth curve as we relate to compatibility, chemistry, and attraction in friendships is creating accountability around our personal weaknesses. This will require profound honesty to confess emotional fusion, intense attraction, sexual energy, or ease of connection to those with whom we are closest. Usually this doesn't seem like the greatest of ideas—to tell the person we're attracted to that we're experiencing impulses or urges that we don't know what to do with or how to handle. A better first step may be to take our concerns to our spiritual director, closest friends, a trusted coworker, or community member. And yes, in some cases, our partners.

Naming our own vulnerabilities forces accountability. Taking our vulnerabilities to those we trust allows us to guide and monitor our blind spots.

THE SURPRISING GIFT IN THE LACK OF CHEMISTRY

Finally, one of the most unlikely gifts of chemistry is when our communities become so large that we don't have an effortless chemistry with some of our coworkers, friends, or fellow community members.

What should you do when you're part of a community, in an organization, or connected to a circle of friends with whom you basically have no chemistry? What should you do when you don't like some of the people you interact with most?

Groups of friends, along with almost every other kind of community that expands, inevitably experience a thinning out. Friends get married and have less time to invest in other relationships. Families are started, limiting people's social space and relational energy. People move away. Major life transitions, such as divorce or career changes, force circles of relationships to morph.

Whatever the case may be, over the years all groups of people experience transitions. People come and go.

Those who stay experience very natural periods of growth and personal change. Sometimes our closest friend may marry someone that we don't find particularly interesting. Even worse, sometimes we plain don't like the partners of some of our dearest companions. Many communities experience periods of growth when new members who join because of common vocational imaginations don't gel relationally with the existing community members.

> Major life transitions, such as divorce or career changes, force circles of relationships to morph.

When such transitions happen, we often experience unintentional layers of division that sneak up on the various "generations" of a group. Though all these differences and different layers of a community add to its textured diversity, making all our relationships more beautiful and inclusive, they can also carry huge potential to disrupt the chemistry of a group.

What should we do when we find ourselves committed to a community that has grown, matured, experienced transitions, and thinned out the original chemistry of its early members?

My current community consists of nearly three hundred staff, board members, interns, and volunteers. We are quite a large group of people who share vocational commitments. But the truth is, there are a few people with whom I just don't connect. In fact, I probably wouldn't be friends with some of our community members if we didn't serve together in the same organization. That's not to say that they're bad people or there's anything wrong with them. Quite the contrary, all those who have joined the community I serve are heroes of hope—men and women who have sacrificed almost everything to fight for justice on behalf of children whose childhood has been plundered.

> The lack of chemistry has been an invitation to find creative connection points.

But the irony of our community becoming more accepting and inclusive is that we often find ourselves desperately searching for far-reaching relational connection points.

This has not become a limiting paradigm, nor have we allowed the lack of chemistry some of us experience to create divisions in our working relationships. We've experienced quite the opposite; the lack of chemistry has been an invitation to find creative connection points where we learn to celebrate our commonality.

In the early stages, when circles of friends or communities are formed, chemistry is a huge factor in drawing people together and keeping them united. But as these relationships mature and make room for others, it's inevitable that chemistry or connections won't always be as effortless as in the beginning.

A few things happen at these stages of maturation. Circles

of friends or communities, in genuine attempts to maintain the purity of energy they share, may become so exclusive that they don't make room for different kinds of people with different kinds of energies. These groups have a tough time growing, both in size and in maturity. They may be some of the circles of people with the strongest bonds, but tragically the gifts of their relationships will never be shared outside their own circle.

Groups who have a vision or sense of self larger than the individuals they're made up of can opt to include anyone and everyone who's interested in joining them. The downside can be that the original factors that brought a group together can become so thinned out that a group becomes uninteresting and uninspiring.

We need to find a way somewhere between these two extremes to protect the energy that unites us around vision or friendship while making room for people who seem to have a hard time fitting in.

When there's someone in a circle of friends or community with whom we don't naturally gel, it can make some of us a little grumpy. We tend to get impatient, set unrealistic expectations, and, at worst, ignore them.

If we want to be in true community, we have to make the choice to not give in to what's easy but instead to explore the unique gifts each person brings. One way to do this is to triangulate on them, working with them or spending time together by including a common friend with whom we both share chemistry. That bridge builder can illuminate for everyone in the smaller, more intimate setting what's hard for us to see on our own.

Often, it's those who share the least amount of natural chemistry who work the best together. It's in these relationships where we are sometimes most able to see beyond ourselves to the larger picture and bigger vision that unites us. These relationships become an illustration of true community.

But they are not easy.

What should we do when a lack of chemistry is so severe that it makes working, worshipping, or serving together nearly impossible?

The danger is that we will become so exclusive that we use unrealistic criteria for inclusion for the sake of protecting or preserving a culture. Making a conscious choice to choose the other—to be open to those who are different—creates possibilities for new kinds of friendships and relationships. It forces us to be imaginative and proactive in taking those relationships to places of stability based on more than instinct, impulse, and chemistry. Our conscious choices for one another will lead us to places of acceptance and respect. It's important to resist the easy option of tolerance, because tolerance can exist without love, honor, and respect. I don't want to merely tolerate those in my life I find difficult to live or serve with; I want to accept their uniqueness and peculiar contributions with affirming respect.

Chemistry—the lack of it or the feeling that it controls us—is part of all friendships and communities. Recognizing this, naming it, growing in self-awareness of its tensions, and submitting these challenges to our community allows chemistry to grow us up and solidify the bonds that unite us. Both too much chemistry and tense incompatibility are unavoidable for all communities, but they are manageable. Honest awareness, acceptance of them as gifts for community, and accountability about our vulnerabilities leads to healthy boundaries and strong communities, whether they be made up of compatible or incompatible members. Together we can discover the unexpected gifts in both.

Ingratitude

Killing Chickens in the Golden City

It is another thing entirely to find the kind of companion that makes the difficult moments in life fade into the midst of laughter or meaning.

—Joan Chittister

Kanchipuram is known as the Golden City of a thousand temples. A spiritual center of Hinduism, it's considered one of the seven sacred cities of India. Though many of the city's medieval temples have been destroyed over the years, it's still packed full of rich history and cultural significance.

Some of the most precious people I know come from Kanchipuram.

While still a teenager, Devi was married to a man she didn't meet until their wedding day, a traditional South Indian arranged marriage. After their wedding, the young couple moved from Kanchipuram to the city of Chennai. Work was hard to come by. The young groom found a job as a day laborer working on construction sites doing masonry. Devi sat on the roadside, stringing tiny jasmine flowers into beautiful floral strands that women tied to their hair.

Their story echoed that of many others: rural migration to an urban center left Devi and her husband struggling on the margins of society. Because they were registered as a low caste with the local government, they were granted a small plot of land where they built a tiny home. The walls of their first house were made of dried palm leaves that they had braided and woven together. The roof was formed of scrap metal. Their little slum was soon filled with the sounds of babies crying and of laughter as their family grew until they had five daughters.

When their children were old enough to work, they forwent school to learn sewing and became quite capable seamstresses. Eventually the three oldest daughters found work at a nearby garment factory, essentially a sweatshop. The three young girls worked six days a week, up to fourteen hours a day, and each earned about twenty dollars a month.

My old flat in Chennai was right across the street from Devi's little house. Every day I'd walk by their little home on my way to and from our neighborhood's bus stop. One morning Devi's youngest daughter stood at the front door of their home and called out to me as I passed. Saluting me with her hand to her forehead she yelled out, "Good morning, Uncle!"

Her greeting compelled me to stop to say hello. I kneeled down so I could look the sweet little eight-year-old girl in the eyes.

"*Un peyarenna?*" What is your name?

She replied, "Prabha."

In broken English, Prabha asked if I would play a game of jacks with her cousins and sister. I agreed. To my surprise, no bouncy rubber ball or set of little metal toy jacks was available. Instead, the girls had gathered a small pile of gray gravel stones to play with. I sat on the ground in a circle of six of the sweetest little ladies in my neighborhood, and was soundly beaten in every game.

That jacks game began a friendship that has become one of the most valuable in my life. As I was away from my own family, Devi took it upon herself to provide maternal love and care for me, usually in the form of big South Indian meals. Prabha and her sisters welcomed me into their family, treating me as a brother. On the many evenings when the electricity in our neighborhood was out, the girls would invite me to their place, where the dim, flickering yellow light of a candle or oil lamp filled their room as we flipped through stacks of old family photos or listened to Tamil music on a rickety transistor radio.

I was engaged to Phileena at the time, and during the years I lived in Chennai, she would visit whenever she could. Prabha's family also welcomed Phileena as another sister, often dressing her up, putting makeup on her, and teaching her contemporary Bollywood dances.

During one of Phileena's trips to India, Prabha's family invited us to visit some of their relatives in Kanchipuram. Though just forty miles from the city, the journey, by local bus, took all afternoon.

Their extended family actually lived outside Kanchipuram, in a neighboring town surrounded by rice paddies. It was hard to believe that anyone could be poorer than Prabha's family, but her aunts and uncles had almost nothing. In spite of their poverty, we spent an enjoyable and memorable day walking through the village, meeting old friends, balancing on the ridges that ran through the rice paddies, and lounging in the afternoon sun together. As evening approached, Prabha's older sisters began preparations for dinner. They didn't have much to work with, but the sisters were determined to make us a typical Kanchipuram meal.

As the girls worked, one of Prabha's cousins, a young man in his twenties, tapped me on the shoulder and motioned for me to follow him around back of his little shack. Pecking in the dirt, searching for something to eat, was a scrawny chicken that would soon be stewed in a pot of yellow curry and served over rice. I grew up in the city and until that day had never seen a chicken slaughtered. I still don't know how he caught the thing, but the bird was no sooner in his hands before he took a small razor blade and slit its throat. The blood spurted everywhere.

He took a wicker basket and placed the dying chicken underneath it, holding the basket down while the bird clucked and violently flapped its wings. Once the dying bird had bled out and stopped twitching, he dropped its carcass into a pot of boiling water to loosen the feathers so they'd come out easier. When the bird was completely defeathered, Prabha's cousin deftly removed the innards, organs, and other unpleasant bits that I hoped we wouldn't later discover in our meal. A large knife resembling a village version of a meat cleaver came out and was used to hack the bird into little cubes, which were then dropped into a pot of curry simmering on a nearby open flame.

Some of the most extravagant meals I've ever eaten were served on the dirt floors of refugee camps in West Africa.

It is from those people that I learned about generosity and celebration. It's amazing how those with the least often give the most. Some of the best parties I've ever attended were in the slums of Peru or villages of Nepal. Some of the most extravagant meals I've ever eaten were served not in Rome or Paris but on the dirt floors of refugee camps in West Africa and that evening on the outskirts of one of India's most sacred cities.

If I'm honest, it's really hard for me to receive such gracious hospitality from people I know are so desperately poor. I sometimes feel guilty. But in many of the world's more traditional cultures, hospitality is one of the most important gifts a family can offer. A good host needs a good guest, so that evening Phileena and I sat on the floor in a tiny village home and dined with family. Our hearts burst with gratitude—gratitude for friendship, for the kindness extended to us by Prabha's relatives, and for the lessons we received that day.

SURPRISED BY GRATITUDE

Years later I was invited to join a group of Christian leaders to reflect on the marks that make and break communities. Christine Pohl, a friend and mentor, had been given a Lilly Endowment grant as part of the endowment's Sustaining Pastoral Excellence initiative. Christine invited twelve pastors, three directors of missional communities, and three professors to join her in the exploration. For several years we met semiannually to tease out the implications of practices that make strong communities. One of the outcomes of those meetings was Christine's book *Living into Community: Cultivating Practices That Sustain Us*.

To prepare for each of our gatherings, the participants were asked to write a two-page essay that would be used to facilitate discussions around the marks of community. Christine framed the discussions by suggesting four practices essential for communities: promise keeping, truth telling, hospitality, and gratitude.

I was surprised to see gratitude on the list. Before we got together to discuss gratitude, I almost considered the suggestion a throwaway. I didn't think gratitude should even be on the list. I could understand how being inhospitable or dishonest or breaking a promise could hurt our friendships and damage community. But ingratitude?

It didn't take long into the discussion for me to understand gratitude to be the most important practice on that list.

I took the discussions back to my community, and we kicked the ideas around and talked through the ways we had failed one another in these practices. We got better at cultivating a spirituality and culture of hospitality. In fact, we eventually made hospitality one of the hidden marks of our community culture that we nurture. Of course, truth telling seems to be an obvious one for communities, but we also learned how to be more honest with one another, even when telling the truth seemed to be the hardest or most humiliating thing. Our commitment to keeping our promises further established trust and helped us make more realistic commitments to one another.

But the conversations around gratitude were hard. Really hard.

Many of us hadn't considered the ways in which ingratitude had created subtle distances among us—forgetting to say "thank you" when someone stayed late, pitched in, or helped complete a big project, or merely thanking each other for common courtesies such as opening a door. Sometimes not saying thank you when a meal tab was covered by a community member or failing to express gratitude for well-prepared meetings caused some of us to judge each other as entitled or ungrateful.

As we talked through these things, it actually opened up some tucked-away wounds. People didn't think they could expect gratitude from one another. Many of us had become so accustomed to the flow of our interpersonal interactions that when we evaluated our culture of gratitude, we were surprised to discover we hadn't done it well.

Sometimes it's easier to remain unaware. Once we named gratitude as a core value, the absence of practicing it became painfully pronounced. When we failed each other with ingratitude, the awareness of it created new problems. Coming to expect gratitude from one another led to subtle resentments when we failed to practice it.

It's tough for communities to admit that they haven't recognized the need to express gratitude. It's even tougher to make a point of nurturing a culture of gratitude without feeling as though we're forcing it.

> I could understand how being inhospitable or dishonest or breaking a promise could hurt our friendships and damage community. But ingratitude?

In our community, we determined to make room to express gratitude in staff meetings and community prayer times, but we still struggled in allowing this commitment to take hold in our culture. Eventually, we decided we needed to name all of the essential cultural values (in addition to gratitude) that we considered to be central to our community's identity.

We spent almost five months meeting to talk through what would eventually become a list of our community's hidden marks of community or cultural commitments. Together we watched the video from the Big Omaha conference talk from Tony Hsieh of Zappos on how his company hires and fires based on its internal culture. We asked Adrian Blake, a friend who teaches social entrepreneurship at Creighton University, to walk us through a process of naming and defining our culture. Everyone in our Omaha community had an equal voice in generating the list of desired values. Everyone's suggestions were considered and voted on, and we eventually reduced the core set of indispensable principles to seven: collaboration, communication, hospitality, inclusion, professionalism, respect, and gratitude.

Now during each of our community members' evaluation processes, we hold one another accountable for not simply expressing but receiving sincere appreciation. We're learning to take notice of one another's gifts and contributions, as well as to better recognize and accept one another's ideas, service, and thoughtfulness. We know we still have a long way to go when we have trouble expressing gratitude or when we fail to receive others' expressions of gratitude well. We're learning that gratitude isn't a throwaway at all. It does indeed make and break community.

MALFORMATIONS OF GRATITUDE

Sitting in a little French café over glasses of red wine, I met with the former director of an international relief organization. He had been in charge of the organization's regional blood drive. Responsible for recruiting blood donors in several states, he was telling me some of his strategies in donor retention. As the director of a nonprofit myself, I hoped he'd illuminate the secrets of keeping a giving community engaged and involved.

One of the programs he had implemented included sending personalized thank-you notes to donors. His office had run a test on twenty thousand of its blood donors, who collectively gave an average of 1.9 blood donations a year. To see if the program would work, those twenty thousand donors had been divided into two groups.

He pulled out a little card that had been sent to one of the groups of ten thousand. A computer program generated little notes that roughly went something like this: "Dear Nikole, thank you for your blood donation on January 17. Last week your blood was used at the University of Nebraska Medical Center during an operation on an eleven-year-old girl hurt in a car accident. She'll be okay, thanks largely to your donation. We invite you to continue donating blood as often as you are able."

After I handed the card back to him, he asked what I thought. My first response was that if I were a blood donor I'd seriously want that kind of thank-you note. Who wouldn't want to know where and how her blood was being used? It was brilliant.

He then informed me that the donors who hadn't received the card had continued giving an average of 1.9 times the following year, while those who had received the cards had increased their giving to 3.5 times a year.

After sharing the success of the program, he again asked what I thought about it. This time I responded with a question: "Does *using* gratitude to get what we want, even good things, take away from the sincerity of it?"

Certainly I don't think that utilizing gratitude as a donor retention strategy is entirely misguided—it's at least sensible. But wouldn't it be better to avoid *using* gratitude to manipulate donors? To create a culture of gratitude that invites donors to engage further without being manipulated?

It's a nuanced response, not one loaded with judgment but one that points to a core motivation and response, one that gets to the heart of gratitude: we can be thankful without *using* our thankfulness to get more of what we want. Gratitude used as a tool can be manipulative and malform the very essence of practicing a posture of thankfulness. To use gratitude as a hustle destroys the beauty of it.

In relationships there will always be exchanges of giving and receiving, many of them unnoticed. But when intentionality or thoughtfulness goes into any of these exchanges, gratitude is the appropriate response. Failing to express thankfulness can be hurtful. Not acknowledging how grateful we are for friendships and the kind gestures offered within them can lead to mild forms of resentment.

We can be thankful without using our thankfulness to get more of what we want.

But we need to go further. More than simply saying "thank you," communities living into a real posture of gratitude transform the way we receive the gifts of community. Gratitude also allows us to give more freely in community.

Gratitude not only fortifies trust by validating sacrifices and gifts of love offered in relationships but lays the foundation of a culture of celebration.

GRATITUDE AND CELEBRATION

When I joined my community, I had no idea what I was getting myself into. I had simply attempted to respond to my own exposure to human suffering. Sometimes I wonder if I missed out on real life, while other times I think I've seen more of what real life really is than I could ever have imagined. My early to midtwenties were spent working with children dying of AIDS. For a few years I went to more grave sites of little kids than I went to maternity wards; I mourned more children's deaths than celebrated the births of my friend's kids.

The fifty corpses I carried out of Mother Teresa's home back in 1993 shaped everything for me. I was wrecked. It seemed impossible to recover from the intensity of those first months in Kolkata, and I don't know that I'd even want to recover if I could. It's usually at a party or when I've met someone and begun telling him or her of those profoundly formational years that I start to glimpse the strangeness of it all.

During those early years of forming community among the suffering, I had to battle the conflicting realities I was trying to hold in tension. I would visit one of our community's international projects, interacting with children forced to prostitute themselves or young boys recruited to fight in an armed conflict, and then fourteen hours later get off a plane and fall into the normalcy of a life in the United States, where many people can't make sense of suffering.

I'm still asked how I live in the "back-and-forth" of working in the context of affluence and comfort while spending so much time fighting for the freedoms and dignity of the exploited and impoverished. I don't know that I have an answer, because I don't know that I really do that part of my life very well.

What I've learned is that celebration is a mark of healthy community. Celebration has to be one of the core components of forming and sustaining relationships. That might sound crazy after all the stories I've told of suffering, betrayal, and loss. But without celebration, how can we live at peace in the world? How can we cultivate friendships with those who seem to know only suffering? Before we can learn how to really celebrate, we have to learn how to suffer.

> Celebration is a mark of healthy community.

This is the unexpected gift we find in our poorest friends. Those gracious, generous hosts who give without restraint. Those welcoming families who slaughter their only chicken for their guest and spend an entire day preparing a never-to-be-forgotten meal.

What is it about those who seem to have the least that allows them to give the most?

In perhaps one of literature's most winsome little books, Khalil Gibran unwraps the mystery of this: "Your joy is your sorrow unmasked. And the selfsame well from which your laughter rises was oftentimes filled with your tears. And how else can it be? The deeper that sorrow carves into your being, the more joy you can contain. Is not the cup that holds your wine the very cup that was burned in the potter's oven? And is not the lute that soothes your spirit, the very wood that was hollowed with knives? When you are joyous, look deep into your heart and you shall find it is only that which has given you sorrow that is giving you joy. When you are sorrowful, look again in your heart, and you shall see that in truth you are weeping for that which has been your delight."[1]

Gratitude and celebration are the fruits of suffering; they are gifts in community that should never be manipulated but honored. In the hollowed-out spaces sorrow carves within us, celebration finds a home.

Tangible reminders of celebration mark many of our deepest relationships. Friends sometimes get tattooed together; married couples exchange rings. In our community, when we commission someone into full-time service, we give him or her a silver San Damiano cross. These symbols are loaded with meaning and become points of return that give us the comfort of being able to express in outward signs what's deep within us that we can't put into words.

> **Gratitude and celebration are the fruits of suffering.**

In addition to the San Damiano cross, we give our friends a little black ring from Brazil. This tradition started years ago with a Brazilian friend, Lília, who first gave us the simple black ring made from the fruit of the tucum palm tree, a plant difficult to cultivate due to its long, thin, sharp thorns. Handmade from the fruit's hard shell that surrounds the seed, it typically takes more than an hour to cut and polish one ring.

Along with her gift, Lília shared a story. She spoke of a bishop who in a meeting with the leaders of the Tapirapé people, an autochthonous tribe, was awed by their faith and resilience. He asked for their forgiveness for the way his people had treated their people. More important, he asked forgiveness for the church's complicity in oppressing their people over the centuries.

The bishop removed his gold ring, the symbol of his liturgical office, and presented the ring to the leader of the community, saying something to the effect of "Though we cannot return all the gold we've plundered or restore all the lives we destroyed, we long to try to make things right. Take this ring as a symbol of my desire for what the church will be—no longer taking but giving."

The Tapirapé chief accepted the ring and reciprocated the bishop's gesture by removing his black tucum ring and giving it to the church leader as a symbol of their forgiveness and in celebration of their newfound solidarity.

The symbolism of the black ring has changed over the years. In the 1800s the ring was a sign of marriage for the slaves and autochthonous people who could not afford to buy gold. It was also a symbol of friendship and of resistance to the established order—the freedom fighters. Today the black ring of tucum has come to symbolize solidarity and the celebration of friendship with those living in poverty.[2]

The tucum ring is a reminder that our friendships cannot remain insulated and isolated in the narrow space of a group of people who share a vocation, worship together, and live like one another. But that friendship, if alive and vibrant, is marked by gratitude and sustained in contagious and creative celebration.

Gratitude moves communities into places of celebration. There's something existential, eternal about celebration. I stated this earlier, but I love the imagery, so I will risk repeating myself: in all of the world's great religions, a banquet is one of the common metaphors used to describe the various understandings of heaven. There's something inside each of us that yearns to be at that table in paradise. The table has become sacramental in my life. At shared meals I experience a foretaste of what we hope is to come, longing for an eternal union with God and our friends. Whether it's a table in our homes or plates set on a dirt floor in Kanchipuram, gratitude prepares us to celebrate the gifts of friendship and community.

Grief

Living Among the Dying

If you do not transform your pain, you will surely transmit it to those around you.

—Richard Rohr

For a second-grade student at a Catholic elementary school in Omaha, Nebraska, life was pretty simple. My parents packed my Star Wars lunch box every morning, so I never went without food. The dress code at my school required a clean light blue button-down shirt with navy blue pants every day, so I never went without clothes. On the weekends, I played Little League baseball at the local YMCA and went to church with my family, so I almost never found myself alone.

My life was ordered, routine, predictable, and safe. While I lived a sheltered and protected life as a second-grade student, 7 million Cambodians suffered unspeakable horrors under the Khmer Rouge regime led by the notorious Pol Pot.

Some observers estimate that as many as 3 million of Cambodia's 7 million people lost their lives during the four-year reign of terror that seized their homeland. For those who survived, their lives were shattered. There were no schools for their children and no clothes for their babies, and many little kids found themselves alone, orphaned by the barbarity inflicted on them by their own neighbors.

Phileena and I have visited Cambodia multiple times. On one of our trips to Phnom Penh we went to Tuol Sleng, also known as S-21. This former high school was the primary interrogation and torture center where almost fifteen thousand innocent people were convicted as "conspirators." In what had once been classrooms, men, women, and children were forced to confess to crimes they had never committed. The forced confessions were induced by unspeakable forms of brutal torture. Those who died during torture were buried in the school grounds. Inmates who survived their torture were taken to the Killing Fields of Choeung Ek.

> While I lived a sheltered and protected life as a second-grade student, 7 million Cambodians suffered unspeakable horrors.

In a rural farming area on the edge of Cambodia's capital city lie what appear to be ordinary rice paddies. However, throughout the fields are numerous mass graves. These are the infamous Killing Fields, where more than twenty thousand innocent people died brutal deaths. The deaths were brutal because the Khmer Rouge needed to save bullets to fight the Vietnamese. Instead of shooting their prisoners, they used hoes, pickaxes, and other common tools to kill the victims, even resorting to live burials. Some of the worst accounts detail their holding little babies by their legs and slamming them into tree trunks to kill them.

As the innocent people of Cambodia suffered through this nightmare, the world turned a deaf ear and blinded itself to the inhumanity of the atrocities. Today a hardened and worn trail makes its way through the memorial at the Killing Fields. Occasionally as you walk on the path, you might notice a bone fragment protruding from the smooth dirt surface. Maybe a leg bone or possibly several spinal vertebrae catch your eye as the sun reflects off the shine of the smooth white bone fragments— the only thing left behind by the silent and forgotten victims. Bits and shreds of clothing still make their way to the surface, unearthed from the more than 112 mass graves located on the site that are yet to be examined and unearthed. With each piece of bone or clothing that surfaces, it's as if the bodies are crying out to be heard and remembered.

As Phileena and I walked through the memorial, we encountered several children begging, playing, and sleeping in the empty, hollowed-out exhumed mass graves that had once held the dead bodies of hundreds of innocent victims. The children were playing among the remains of the men, women, and children. Skeleton fragments were all that was left, some of the skulls still bearing the blindfolds they had been forced to wear during their executions.

Not much has changed since Pol Pot's Khmer Rouge devastated Cambodia. Today children play, live, and die in the killing fields of the modernized world. Today more than twelve thousand children will die preventable deaths simply because of a lack of proper nutrition. Today in places such as Darfur, the Congo, Angola, Kashmir, Indonesia, Iraq, Sri Lanka, Chechnya, North Korea, Israel, Palestine, and Afghanistan children continue to play in the hollowed-out graves of those who can't or won't work out their differences. Today innocents, including vulnerable children, suffer at the hands of grave injustice.

And all the while the world continues to turn deaf ears and blind eyes.

Remembering the tragedy of the Khmer Rouge and the legacy of the Killing Fields should inspire us to work to bring an end to suffering and injustice today.

It is a sick world, not really a safe place for those who are desperately poor. Instead of turning away, we can face these tragedies and injustices by allowing them to wash over us with a bath of grief—an initiation to suffer with our brothers and sisters.

LOSING CHILDHOOD IN A CEMETERY

When I moved to India, I spent the afternoons of my first week just poking around, exploring my new neighborhood. About a half mile down the road from my apartment was the Kilpauk Cemetery. I had never seen anything like it.

High concrete walls surround the property, preventing people from seeing graves from the street. The entrance is a twenty-foot-high black iron barred gate. Somehow more than fifty thousand people are buried there, their graves stacked almost on top of one another. The first time I visited the Kilpauk Cemetery, I walked all the way to the back, where, then at least, there was still an unused patch of green grass.

Today innocents, including vulnerable children, suffer at the hands of grave injustice.

That cemetery was the first quiet place I had found in the city. Part of me thought that I'd probably spend a lot of time at the back of that cemetery, enjoying the quiet, sitting in the sun, and reading or writing letters home. But after just a few moments I noticed several little kids running around the grave sites, malnourished children from a nearby slum, playing among the dead. The imagery was too much for me, and I didn't go back to that graveyard until we began burying our children from the Word Made Flesh homes there.

Sadly, in just two years' time we buried ten of our little friends in that cemetery—little girls and one tiny boy who died from complications due to AIDS. Children we named. Kids we considered family. Each of the losses was devastating. Watching children die slow, agonizing deaths has to be one of the worst things imaginable.

I have the name of one of those little girls tattooed on my left arm.

Although much smaller than other children her age, Suryakala holds a huge place in my heart. Her name meant "Little Princess of the Sun." Suryakala had a tremendous impact on me and everyone else who met her. Her soft, quiet voice was singsong perfect. Her eyes were beautiful and full of life. Her smile was tender, innocent, and pure.

Her body was terribly weak, but Suryakala embodied strength. Due to complications from AIDS, she died a few weeks before what would have been her tenth birthday. Phileena and I last saw her just weeks before her death. She looked great. The antiretroviral prescription she was taking had helped her so much. I remembered clearly how sick she had been and celebrated her dramatic health improvements. I hoped for the future that could be hers and grieved for the childhood she had lost. Sadly, days after our visit, she took a drastic turn for the worse.

I had first met her seven years earlier, when she was just three years old. She had tuberculosis, and I remember holding her frail body against my chest to try and keep her warm. Every time she coughed, her entire frame shook. She was so weak she could hardly hold her head up. I left Chennai back then, fearful I would never see her again, believing her sickness would overcome her. To my surprise, not only did she recover, but she seemed quite healthy and her little body began to grow.

Phileena and I spent a lot of time with Suryakala each time we visited India. She had lost her mother to AIDS, and her father was very sick with the disease when he brought his two daughters to our children's homes. Shortly after she joined us, Surya's father succumbed to the disease. Phileena and I were in Chennai at that time and spent as much time as we could with Surya and her older sister. During the time of grieving and mourning with them, my love for these sisters deepened.

I count it one of the greatest privileges of my life to have seen Surya grow from an undernourished little girl to a thriving nine-year-old, grieving with her during the loss of her father and making memories that are now cherished treasures. I imagine her now, full of health and life, in the loving arms of God. I imagine her surrounded by the countless other children whose lives have been tragically cut short. I imagine her reunited with the others from the home who went before her: Esther Noel, Ragini, Abraham, Poornima, baby Sarah, Prema . . . other children whose lives ended far too soon.

Today a small, whitewashed concrete cross bears Surya's name. The cross rests with her remains in the Kilpauk graveyard, where she is surrounded by her brothers and sisters. All those little white crosses are a memorial that reminds and compels us to continue to fight for the lost childhood of nations of children.

In Surya's life, she was perfect in her uniqueness. In her death, she lives on as a symbol of hope for the millions of other children like her who suffer today. And for us,

I imagine Surya now, full of health and life, in the loving arms of God.

Surya's death is a prophetic reminder of the thousands who will fall this day, passing without a tear—children who won't have a grave one can visit or friends who mourn their deaths. Every one of the Word Made Flesh children who have died leaves a painful mark deep in my soul, but Suryakala's death is a wound that I continue to grieve.

THE GIFT OF GRIEF IN SAYING YES

Even before Phileena and I were married, we began making lists of the names we would bestow on our own future children. While we were engaged, I started buying gifts for what I hoped would be our future family. In South India I found a gorgeous little purple floral-print dress for our first daughter, and in Nepal I bought a dark green wool jacket that we would give to our first son.

We had both grown up in amazing homes with incredible parents. Neither of us had experienced any trauma or abuse in our childhoods. Both sets of our parents had remained married, and we both had some of the best siblings anyone could ask for. Everything in our lives had prepared us for parenthood.

It was the childhoods of our new friends, kids like Suryakala, that caused us to rethink what family meant.

On our honeymoon, Phileena and I started to map out what we thought would be the schedule of beginning our own family. We had planned to wait at least a year before trying to conceive a baby. But by the end of that year the weight of suffering and the subsequent needs of the children we worked with were so overwhelming that we considered delaying having our own children.

The closer we got to kids in India, Nepal, Sierra Leone, Romania, and Peru, the further away the hopes of our own children went. It wasn't that saying "yes" to children of our own would mean "no" to the kids we had already made commitments to. But a "yes" to our own kids would change the hard "yeses" we had already made. Some of those "yeses" were to children who had already lost so much, and another loss would have been devastating.

Phileena and I actually spent a good eight years praying, fasting together, seeking counsel from trusted friends and proven mentors. We knew that having children of our own would change our life drastically. It would mean grieving for some of the freedoms we had as a childless couple. But more than that, it would mean grieving for some of the ways we had made ourselves available to children all over the world.

We also realized that saying no to having children of our own would mean grieving for the possibilities of family, the miracle of conception, and growing old with daughters or sons.

During our process of discernment, we considered adoption. Had it been possible to bring Suryakala into our home, we would have. So when she died, it felt as though part of us died with her.

Eventually Phileena and I decided to remain childless. That

was the hardest decision either of us has ever made. I would be lying if I didn't admit that living with the decision brings tremendous sadness, especially when I'm around vibrant, happy families. Coming to that decision wasn't something God asked us to do, but I believe God gave us the grace to make the sacrifice.

> **That decision wasn't something God asked us to do, but I believe God gave us the grace to make the sacrifice.**

Some people didn't understand. Some thought we were just being selfish. Others explained that we were disobeying God's command to "bear fruit, increase your numbers, and fill the earth" (Genesis 1:28). Though everyone had an opinion about our decision, we quietly grieved, and still do grieve, for the sacrifice we've made.

Though it's still difficult at times, we're confident that we made the right decision. The pain we live with doesn't make us reconsider our decision; rather, it reminds us of the continued sacrifices we've committed to. And sometimes grief follows sacrifice. Making that sacrifice has allowed us to continue living our lives for the plundered childhood of many of our little friends, younger brothers and sisters for whom we fight.

LIVING AMONG THE DYING

Thankfully, we're part of a community that tries to understand. Our community grieves with us. Many of those in our community understand the reasons we've made this decision.

When you live among the dying, the way you relate to your own freedoms is turned upside down. In Word Made Flesh, it's not uncommon for our friends to die of AIDS, police violence, street fights, or domestic abuse. We live in a world that cries for mercy, for justice. The brokenness of the world has been an invitation not only to face but also to tend to the wounds in God's heart. In the face of suffering, injustice, and oppression, we have found a fight to break up—the fight between the integrity of God's character and the powers that try to discredit that integrity. The courageous energy that breaks up the fight is our collective commitment to embodying the goodness of God's nature, which seems to be absent in so many parts of the world.

As a community, we grieve the loss of our friends. When we began to gather content for the twentieth-anniversary edition of our community's publication, we wanted to include a memorial section. With so much to celebrate after twenty years of faithful service, we needed to make space to grieve for those who hadn't lived to see our anniversary. So I wrote each of our international communities and asked them to begin to assemble the lists of memorials we would include from their locations.

The number was staggering.

While visiting one of our teams in South America, our field director told me she couldn't remember everyone—she said there were well over a hundred women and children who had died since she started working. When our anniversary publication did go to print, we were able to include only sixty memorials, each of them for friends we still grieve.

> When you live among the dying, the way you relate to your own freedoms is turned upside down.

Naively, I used to think that community was the answer to grief. I used to think that suffering together would reduce or mitigate the pain of loss, but I discovered that suffering in community enhances the pain we feel. This happens at funerals. For example, a grandparent might unexpectedly pass away. Though sad and tragic in its own right, most people expect to outlive their grandparents. Based on their temperament or their nearness to a loved one, people process and experience the loss of a grandparent differently. And when a group of people comes together at a funeral to grieve that loss, somehow it's as if the emotion becomes more real, enhanced by the shared grief of friends and family.

Community may create a layer of much-needed support as we grieve together, but contemplative spirituality is what sustains us. Contemplative prayer practices help us become much more accepting of ourselves, others, and the things we can't control.

Grief must be accepted. We can't control it; we have to experience the depths of grief. In a contemplative posture we are able to receive the pain as a gift filled with healing and lament. Contemplative spirituality prepares us to face grief. But what is contemplative spirituality?

For me it's become a journey of consent, a way of letting go of the things I try to control.

My friend Andrew Marin used to play college baseball. Professional teams such as the Mets, Marlins, and Pirates were considering drafting him out of college. So I asked him, "How does somebody get *that good* at baseball?"

He told me that every day he would set up a batting tee in his parents' garage and hit a tennis ball a hundred times or so. The repetitious practice of swinging the bat wasn't so much about building the muscles needed to swing. Rather, it was more about building the muscle memory to solidify the perfect swing. He was training himself to remember how a perfect swing felt.

I would have thought he'd need to practice swinging at moving balls. During games he would face pitches coming at him at nearly 100 miles per hour. But getting timing down and attaining a perfect swing were much more complicated than I realized.

That illustration of unglamorous, patient practice has stuck with me as a symbol of contemplative practice or discipline.

In our community, we give ourselves in relationship to grassroots movements toward justice. We locate ourselves in some of the forgotten corners of the world: red-light areas, refugee camps, favelas and slum communities, and neighborhoods known more for their criminal activities than for their hospitality. We live and serve among people victimized by human trafficking, former child combatants, women and children exploited by the commercial sex industry, populations of youth who live and work on the streets, and children who have been orphaned because their parents had AIDS or who are HIV-positive themselves. Collectively we bear witness to hope—the possibility that God is good in a world that has legitimate reasons to question God's goodness.

It often feels as though we have 100-mile-an-hour fastballs of poverty, despair, loss, and violence flying at our heads. In the face of such suffering, many of my prayers become demands for God to fix the problems our friends battle over and over. Many of my prayers plead with God to take the pain from my heart. This is a spirituality of activism at its best—active prayers in the midst of an intensely active life of service among the suffering.

In our community we talk about contemplative activism, but we haven't always described ourselves as contemplative activists. The contemplative part has emerged only over the past few years. Before we discovered the need for a contemplative basis for our activism, we saw many staff members teeter on the edge of burnout. We lost a number of good people to exhaustion and grief.

We didn't know how to accept grief as a gift.

Cultivating the contemplative basis for our active life hasn't been easy. It's meant stopping our activity and evaluating where its motivation originates. It's meant creating rhythms for rest, Sabbath, and sabbatical. It's meant placing value on a communal praxis of reflection that allows space for members to examine and process the pace, successes, failures, and contributions we make in service, as well as the grief we experience. It's meant learning to care for ourselves and nurture rules of life that allow us to thrive in mission. It's meant learning about and practicing many of the church's historical contemplative prayer practices, such as lectio divina, the breath prayer, the examen, and centering prayer.

> That illustration of unglamorous, patient practice has stuck with me as a symbol of contemplative practice or discipline.

Centering prayer asks for twenty minutes of silence. Rather than actively formulating prayers, petitions, or requests, centering prayer is *active consent* to the divine presence of God. It's a prayer practice of letting go of the mind's desire to control and cultivating awareness and presence. When I make the time for it, I notice something interesting: the fruit of the prayer becomes a form of muscle memory. I'm learning how to consent.

I'm learning to consent not only to the work of God in my own soul but also to what seems to be God's pace of service. The grace of consent moves my prayers away from demands on God to a peaceful faith that God will illuminate a better way. My contemplative muscle memory allows me to stay in the grief of lost loved ones instead of pushing it away in an effort to fix what I find wrong with the world.

The more I make contemplative prayer practices a central part of my spiritual formation, the more able I am to face the 100-mile-an-hour fastballs heading my way. Yes, this practice often feels undramatic and of course goes unnoticed, but discovering the contemplative basis for activism has given us the gift of a muscle memory that produces peace.

I never expected that I would have to learn to live with so much death. The bodies I've carried out of Mother Teresa's home and the countless little children we've buried since then stay with me. Every so often, when I hold a glass of wine, I look at my hand. Is it really possible that the same hands that have held the dying, carried the corpses of children, and wiped away the tears of the suffering are permitted to raise a glass of wine and toast with friends?

> I'm learning to consent not only to the work of God in my own soul but also to what seems to be God's pace of service.

Every year I visit that graveyard in Chennai, India. I'll sometimes spend an hour or so going from one little white cross to the next. I lay rose petals and strands of jasmine flowers on each grave as I say a prayer for my friends, both those who've passed away and those who still suffer through life.

I don't know why I'm still surprised by my response, but each time I visit the graves of my little sisters and brother in Kilpauk, I break down. The tears are a reminder of the loss of life and love, a loss I don't think God wanted. The tears bathe my face and fall on the graves of girls and boys whose lives and deaths remind me of the things I've withheld and the costs I've incurred to be available to them. My tears are prayers, each one an invitation to love more deeply as I throw myself on the mercy of a world in need of peace.

Grief has no easy solutions, but contemplative spirituality helps us receive the hidden gifts tucked away in the broken places of our hearts. Accepting grief doesn't mean that we concede what's wrong in the world, but it does challenge us to live more intentionally into the possibility of hope. Our experiences of grief remind us of what needs healing and draw us into the idea that our sacrifices could possibly be the answers to someone's prayer for hope.

Maybe even our own.

Restlessness

Faithful in the Undramatic

Be faithful in small things because it is in them that your strength lies.

—Mother Teresa

B angkok is one of my favorite cities in the world. Its pulsing energy, rich culture, fabulous food, and historical and religious heritage make Bangkok one of a kind. It's one of those rare places where East meets West, where rich and poor live smashed together, and where progressive modernization collides with conservative tradition. And, like every big city, it has its social justice issues; its commercial sex industry is notorious worldwide. You can buy anything you want in this city, from sex to electronics to anything you can imagine branded Hello Kitty.

Since the early 1990s, I've traveled to the city nearly thirty times, and on each visit there's one special place I make sure to go.

I am like a diva when it comes to my pens. On the rare occasion I don't use red ink, you might catch me using an obscure variant of blue. The wad of pens I tuck in my carry-on luggage and those stashed away in my office desk drawer come primarily from a bookstore in Bangkok. When I'm in town, I make sure to drop by the shop and load up on hard-to-find Japanese and Korean pens.

Once, after plundering the pen kiosk, I decided to poke around the shelves of books at the back of the store. A thin novel with a soft blue cover jumped out at me. I pulled the volume off the shelf and began reading the back cover. When I started reading it later that week, I don't remember putting that book down.

The Housekeeper and the Professor by Yoko Ogawa is a winsome and sad Japanese tale about a brilliant math professor who, following a traumatic accident, lives with a short-term memory that lasts only eighty minutes. The professor's guardian employs a housekeeper from a temp agency. The young woman, a single mom, sometimes has to bring her son to work at the professor's house. As the book unfolds, it's a tragically beautiful story of love in the most undramatic of circumstances. Every morning, the young housekeeper and her son have to reintroduce themselves to the professor. If her errands, running to the market or the post office, take longer than eighty minutes, she's forced to start all over in building trust with the professor.

> One of the hardest but most beautiful breakthroughs in life is finding meaning in the mundane.

The one she serves forgets her every day. Even so, knowing she'll be forgotten, she continues to give the best of herself.

In this charming little story we discover the difficulty of faithfulness in the mundane. Just think of the dazzling, deep discoveries we'd find if only we had the fortitude in our friendships, communities, or vocations to keep showing up, even when it's unappreciated or unnoticed.

One of the hardest but most beautiful breakthroughs in life is finding meaning in the mundane. This may take years, but the gifts of fidelity during periods of boredom strengthen the bonds of relationships and solidify our life's purpose.

PRAYING THE WORK: A VOCATION OF THE MUNDANE

When I was a kid, I thought I knew what I wanted to be when I grew up. I went to first and second grade at Saint Bernard's Catholic School, and from that very early age, I felt an internal urge toward the priesthood. There was something about a vocation devoted to God that drew me.

While I was still in elementary school, my parents decided to leave the Catholic Church and became Protestant. Of course, I didn't really have a say in which Christian faith tradition I was raised in, but even as a little guy, the bit about celibacy for Catholic clergy made me have second thoughts about the religious life. I also found the Protestant service much longer but easier to sleep through since there was far less standing, kneeling, and sitting. So the move to Protestantism was a welcome one. As I grew up, the vibrancy of my Christian experience reopened my childhood inclinations toward serving the church.

I began my university studies thinking that I'd graduate with a degree in biblical studies or theology and then go on to seminary. But, as in most of life's stories, a dramatic interruption arrested my vocational course, derailing it and reorienting me toward people living in abject poverty.

My junior year at university was spent in Israel at a school on Mount Zion in Jerusalem. I had taken a semester abroad, studying, among other things, biblical Hebrew, Islamic thought and practice, and archaeology. Every afternoon after class, I'd head off campus into the Old City of Jerusalem and get lost down one of the countless passageways or tangled alleys that make up the city.

Those meandering afternoons were laden with intense and inescapable exposure to some of the poorest people I had ever met. A Palestinian student and I spent a lot of time poking around the Old City, and I frequently found myself watching while he was frisked against the stone walls of the city or indiscriminately harassed by the Israel Defense Forces (young men roughly the same age as we were).

Sometimes I'd walk down to the Hinnom Valley to kick a soccer ball around with internally displaced Palestinian children—kids who should have been in school but lacked access to a basic thing like education. Other times I'd just find an interesting place to sit near the Damascus Gate or by the Via Dolorosa and drink in the vitality of an international city bustling with life.

On those afternoons, elderly, blind, or disabled people approached me with open palms and persistent pleas. That semester in Jerusalem included some of my earliest interactions with people begging, something that has become a recurring theme in my life and is still one of the most complex scenarios I routinely find myself navigating.

All of that exposure to poverty was overwhelming. I didn't have the framework to understand what I encountered in Israel. Sure, I had seen poverty while growing up in Omaha, but the systemic oppression in Israel aggravated the poverty there in ways I couldn't wrap my mind around.

All of that awoke something within me. In one of the most serendipitous exchanges of my life, Logiro, a fellow student from rural Uganda, let me borrow Dominique Lapierre's *The City of Joy*. Logiro had been a safe conversation partner as I verbally processed what I was seeing in Jerusalem. With the demands of my classes I found it tough to find time to read anything else, but I had to give it a go. I slogged my way through a few chapters, but once I got past the first fifty pages, the book had me. I devoured it.

The City of Joy tells two simultaneous stories: one of a Polish priest who moves into a Kolkata slum in an attempt to discover Christ amidst poverty; the other of a rural Indian farmer who becomes the tragic face of urban migration and ends up in the same slum as the priest. The weaving of their lives creates a narrative of pain and hope, triumph and disgrace. In vivid detail, the book takes the reader into the heart of urban poverty in India. It's profoundly devastating.

> I didn't have the framework to understand what I encountered in Israel.

All those things created a deep restlessness in me. I wanted to find places and communities of hope among the suffering of the world. So the summer between my junior and senior year at university, I spent a few months poking around Asia. Looking for conversation partners and communities of hope, I traveled through Korea, Malaysia, Singapore, Thailand, Nepal, and Bangladesh.

For the first time I was welcomed into slums and experienced the generosity of people who seemed so poor they had nothing to give. Making my last stop in India, I gingerly knocked on the door of the Mother House, the convent where Mother Teresa and the Missionaries of Charity lived, and signed up to volunteer.

My vocation had found me and wouldn't let go.

Throughout my first weeks in Kolkata, I had a number of opportunities to meet with Mother Teresa. Those encounters only fortified my vocational urges. Mother would speak to me of calling and service, always bringing our conversations back to Christ and our need to look for him among those in poverty. She would frequently say, "Pray the work."

Pray the work?

That phrase replayed itself over and over in my mind as I was volunteering in the Home for the Dying. I had all these notions of what working with the Missionaries of Charity would be—noble and idealistic assumptions that my benevolent availability would be a game changer for people who are poor. However, the reality was sobering. Most of my time serving alongside the Missionaries of Charity looked like scrubbing floors, washing dishes, or doing laundry by hand.

> The challenge is to be faithful and consistent, "praying the work" when no one is looking.

It didn't take long to find opportunities to "pray the work" as a way to give meaning to the undramatic tasks that filled my days. All my romanticized ideas of international volunteerism were quietly dismantled by the seemingly endless to-do list of mundane and ordinary assignments.

Most of real life consists of living in the ordinary, in-between times, the space and pauses filled with monotony. Most of real life is undramatic. The challenge is to be faithful and consistent, "praying the work" when no one is looking or when there's no recognition of our contributions.

FROM "PRAY THE WORK" TO PRAYERS THAT DON'T SEEM TO WORK

In the late 1960s and early '70s the Cistercian monk Father Thomas Keating noticed a trending surge toward contemplative spirituality. He lamented that many of those exploring contemplative prayer practices were going to ashrams or turning to Hinduism or Buddhism for instruction rather than seeking direction from cloistered Christian communities in monasteries or convents. For centuries, Christians have committed themselves to the rich historical tradition of contemplative spirituality, but most of those communities were tucked away, far removed from the average layperson. That inspired Father Keating to establish Contemplative Outreach, a movement to encourage contemplative spirituality and prayer practices for normal people in their everyday lives.

It was a brisk fall morning when I got a call from my spiritual director. Bob had been a high-powered, successful lawyer until an accident left him paralyzed from the neck down. Confined to a wheelchair, he had gone inward, searching out the vast and unexplored spaces of his soul through centering prayer. He had received the gift of his wheelchair as his own personal monastery.[1] Bob and I would occasionally meet for periods of silence. So when he called and invited me to join him for a private dinner with Father Keating, I was eager to meet one of his mentors.

That dinner blew my mind, and from that moment forward the gift of contemplative spirituality was passed along from Father Thomas Keating to our community. Father Keating was speaking at a conference at Creighton University in Omaha. The format was compelling: he would lecture, then lead the conference participants in a contemplative prayer sit. We'd debrief the prayer practice and then spend time doing questions and answers.

Though at the time contemplative spirituality was new to Phileena and me, many of those who came to hear Father Keating had nurtured contemplative spirituality for years. During one of the Q&A periods an older woman walked up to the standing microphone to pose her question. She began by sharing how invigorating centering prayer had been for her. She expressed how, when she had initially started cultivating the prayer practice as a discipline, God had seemed strikingly near. She spoke of the gifts emerging in her faith and how much the prayer resonated with her soul. And then she paused, pressed her fingers against her lips, and started sobbing.

As she tried to hold back her tears, almost confessionally, with painful honesty, she explained that she had lost the life in the prayer practice. It had become routine and difficult. It seemed to have no benefit or fruit. By that point she was weeping, pleading with the monk for answers. What had she done wrong? What was she missing? She had experienced almost thirty years of dry, unsatisfying prayers. As she poured her heart out, the room tensed. Hundreds of people in the auditorium felt her pain. The eyes of many in the crowd filled with tears.

I will never forget Father Keating's response. As he listened to the heartbroken cry of this faithful woman, a wide smile spread across his face, cutting new wrinkles into his already aged countenance. She took a moment to pull herself together after finishing. He waited. The pause between her question and his answer seemed pregnant with possibilities. What would he say? What would be the secret of this spiritual master to this eager devotee?

His words were simple, kind, shocking. He looked directly at her and replied, "That is one of the most beautiful things I've ever heard. The gift of the prayer is your intention in making it. This is one of the purest expressions of true love. That you would give yourself faithfully to something, to someone, that apparently gives you absolutely nothing in return. I encourage you to continue praying the same way you have all these years."

Contemplative prayer practices may be one of the most undramatic or mundane disciplines we can give ourselves to. But the gifts of contemplative spirituality carry us into the most ordinary and restless parts of our lives.

WADING THROUGH THE MURKY
WATERS OF BOREDOM IN VOCATION

Mother's advice to "pray the work" and Keating's encouragement to keep praying when we experience nothing in return are eruptions of faithfulness. These examples of faithfulness to monotony and to things that stoke restlessness in us can be hard to process. This realization has been devastating for many of my fellow community members. Lots of people have joined international Christian communities, thinking that as a "professional Christian" involved in cross-cultural, international service among those living in poverty, their lives would be a perpetual experience of being needed and useful. But most of what we do actually goes unnoticed and unappreciated and is entirely undramatic.

Although we should know better, many of us are surprised when we encounter boredom in our communities, relationships, and vocations. We are surprised when we find ourselves living restless, discontented lives. We want more. We want meaning. We want to be part of things that are significant and vocations that make a difference.

Those impulses actually speak to vocation, and we would do well to listen to them. What moves us, excites us, enrages us, makes us weep, or fills us with passion? Those involuntary physiological impulses point to something deep within us. Those visceral reactions can help us discover our vocations or our callings. In the midst of vocational faithfulness, there will be long periods of what seem to be deeply unsatisfying times marked by difficult or unexciting duties or responsibilities.

> Many of us are surprised when we encounter boredom in our communities, relationships, and vocations.

It's during those dry times, those painful periods of boredom or frustration, that we see what we're really made of. Some of us give in and jump to the next most exciting thing, only to realize that the excitement there also wears thin. Until we awaken to the need for vocational fidelity in the hard times, many of us live in serial transitions, or live like career-change junkies, always needing a more intense vocational "hit" to hold our attention.

Ask anyone who's bought an old home. It's a lot of work. Old houses take a lot of attention and can be the source of quite a bit of frustration. You can't give up when the roof leaks or the water heater goes out. For a home to become livable, a commitment is required to both the potential and the possibilities. Having a home also requires faithfulness to all the undramatic tasks we find waiting for us every day: taking out the trash, dusting bookshelves, changing lightbulbs, changing the water in the fishbowl, feeding the dog, paying the utility bills, and all the little things that go into living in our homes.

Parenting may be one of the most undramatic vocations of all. Ask a young stay-at-home parent what goes into his or her days. Sure, little kids are supercute, say the funniest things, and are great to be around. But as a nonparent, I may have some romanticized ideas of what goes into raising a little kid—I mean, how awesome would it be to wake up every morning and get to hang out with children all day?

I love playing with kids. But parenting is much, much more than just playing with kids. What I'm frequently reminded of by friends with young children is a litany of all the difficult and unappreciated demands implicit in parenting. I don't have to change their diapers, weather their tantrums, wake up in the middle of the night to their crying, put the pieces back together after a sugar crash, or tear the house apart looking for a missing shoe. Without faithfulness in the ordinary, mundane roles required of parents, we'd all be a mess (or much more of a mess than we currently are).

As a parent, when things get tough you just can't pick up and move or change out your kids for new ones. Once you've said "yes," you're committed. The unlikely gifts of being committed and staying take a while to discover, but once realized they are some of the most deeply satisfying experiences of life.

I can't count how many times I've heard a community member say, "I'm just unhappy" or "I'm having a hard time finding joy in what I'm doing here." I've had those same feelings. Certainly they are fair and honest statements that speak to authentic experiences. Often these sentiments are important realizations for people in discerning when a vocational or community transition is necessary. Typically though, they become the ruts that fortify patterns. They become habit-forming rationalizations that people use to allow themselves to jump from relationship to relationship, and we see a lot of people moving from church to church, community to community, or job to job, looking for something different. Sadly, they usually find the same thing and experience the same unsatisfying emotions. Sometimes they're even more desolate because their expectations of "the new" had caused them to leave something that wasn't so bad after all. Something they eventually long to return to.

> Once you've said "yes," you're committed.

BECOMING THE ORDINARY
VERSION OF WHO WE ARE

Praying the work and cultivating contemplative spirituality are some of the best illustrations of how the undramatic leads us to deep places of peace in discovering our vocations. These things enable us to make lasting commitments to place and community and awaken us to a clearer recognition of our true identity.

The false self within us wants to inflate our perceptions of who we are, what we should be doing, how we can control our vocational expressions better. The unconscious motivations of our false selves, exposed through contemplative spirituality, pressure us to be people of significance, importance, or value.

This reminds me of a conversation between Jean Vanier and Samuel Wells, the former chaplain at Duke University. Sam had the privilege of meeting Vanier for breakfast. Vanier has given his life in selfless service among some of our world's most vulnerable people, adults with mental disabilities. In 1964, Jean Vanier moved into a small house with two men, Raphaël and Philippe. The two men had been institutionalized because of their developmental disabilities. Vanier wanted to offer them something different, a home. That first home in Trosly-Breuil, France, launched L'Arche, a worldwide movement birthing hundreds of places of peace where communities learned to serve one another.

Curious about the strains on such a demanding vocation, Wells asked Vanier what the hardest part of his vocation was. He anticipated an answer suggesting the weariness of working with people.

Vanier's reply? "If you really want to know, the hardest part is when young people come from college, and they stay with us for a summer, or maybe for a year. And they say, 'This has been the most amazing experience of my life—I've learnt to see the world so differently and value things so truly and ponder things so deeply.' They say it's been transformative. And then they leave. And I think, 'If it's all been so fantastic and transformative, why are you leaving?'"[2]

I've heard a similar version of those sentiments more times than I want to remember. Over our community's past twenty years we've seen hundreds of people join us on four-month internships, as well as staying with us for fifteen or more years. Many of them have found a home among us, many of them have discovered their vocation, yet they can't get past their own restlessness. They want to keep chasing down the next experience that they think will help them discover more of themselves.

In that honest and intimate conversation with Vanier, Wells responded, "Ah, but don't you see, if life is fundamentally the accumulation of experiences, you have to leave, otherwise you'd have to rethink your whole life."

Ever so gently Vanier replied, "Oh, so people leave because they're frightened of who they're becoming if they stay."[3]

> Becoming the best versions of ourselves often requires that we stay.

Becoming the best versions of ourselves often requires that we stay. Stay when things get hard. Stay when we get bored. Stay when we experience periods of unhappiness. Stay when the excitement wears off. Stay when we don't like those we're in community with. Stay when we fail or are betrayed. Stay when we know who we can become if we have courage to be faithful in the undramatic.

PEBBLES AND A PRESIDENCY

The same year Jean Vanier moved into a home with Raphaël and Philippe, another great man was beginning another transformative movement. Nelson Mandela was sent to Robben Island in the winter of 1964. For eighteen years Mandela slept on the floor of a tiny prison cell. He was given a bucket to use for a toilet and a hammer that he used to break large stones into piles of gravel. The men he was incarcerated with became family, but they constantly came and went, creating a fragile sense of stability.

Mandela was cut off from his family, limited to one visitor a year and a single letter every six months. During those eighteen long, tedious years, he allowed for the painful ordinariness of his days to nurture character. Breaking his back over a pile of stones, breaking boulders down to pebbles, developed a faithfulness that created one of Africa's, if not the world's, greatest leaders. It's almost absurd to suggest that eighteen years in a rock quarry made Mandela the president that he was, but without those years I imagine he could have never drummed up the intestinal fortitude to become the man he did.

> All of us will find ourselves responsible for living faithfully within our communities and vocations.

When I visited Robben Island, I toured the rock quarries Mandela had labored in, and to this day I keep a photo of his little prison cell on my desk. The image of his home of eighteen years is an invitation to faithfulness. When I get frustrated with the mundane and routine bits of life, I am reminded that pounding rocks into gravel makes us who we are. Breaking down large, heavy stones into sand and chalky powder creates within us the faithfulness required to live beautifully into the dramatic, while grounding ourselves in the ordinary.

Many of us will never find ourselves incarcerated and most of us will never be elected head of state, but all of us will find ourselves responsible for living faithfully within our communities and vocations.

A Final Word

It was a Monday night and unseasonably warm for late winter. The House of Loom is usually closed on Monday, but one of the owners had opened it for a few friends. Smoke from a few burned-out incense sticks hung in the air, lingering like a prayer. I sat there with the owner as we discussed some difficult places we were finding ourselves in, elbows on a bar table, my hands pressed against my forehead to hold my tired head up.

My head had been hanging low for quite a while. Both the owner and I had hit a wall. Friendships and relationships weren't playing out how we had hoped. I had messed up again, hurting some of those closest to me, and was at a breaking point. It felt as though it would be easier to just walk away from the relationships, to start over. But easier is almost never better, and I knew I had a lot of work to do.

Why bother? Why stick it out when it's hard? Why search for the courage to own my mistakes and work to make them right? Why stay and face the consequences?

As we finished our drinks and wound down an intimate and confessional conversation, we both knew what we had to do.

Staying in tough places meant we'd have to keep learning to love our friends and communities in fresh and dynamic ways.

_____

Easier is almost never better, and I knew I had a lot of work to do.

_____

That night, the House of Loom was a sanctuary, a refuge. It wasn't in a church or in a community center that I found hope, but sitting in a bar facing my humanity and discovering hope in an unlikely spot. I left that night knowing I'd make it, knowing that I'd be supported by friends, and knowing that the community I needed would help me find my way home.

So now, as we strive toward faithfulness, may we throw ourselves on the mercy of community, allowing our lives to be woven together to create vibrant tapestries of hope.

Let our failures further unite us, illuminating the hidden beauty within us.

May our doubts lead to greater faith.

Let us never become so isolated that we lose the fragrance of the blossoms under our very noses.

May isolation expose our divisions and lead us to healing and wholeness.

Let our transitions be grace-filled, accepting, and honest.

May we come to truly know ourselves, receiving the beauty and terror of our humanity.

Let our love not lead to betrayal.

May we find better ways to negotiate chemistry and compatibility without losing one another or ourselves along the way.

Let our gratitude be sustained, leading us away from unspoken resentments.

May we never forget to celebrate, even as we grieve.

May we live faithfully in the undramatic—the incubator of our imaginations—bearing witness to hope . . .

And in discovering the unexpected gifts of shared space, live the way of community.

Acknowledgments

As a child, Donkey Kong was one of my favorite video games. But if you have ever gone old school and actually played the game, you may have found yourself asking, "Where's the donkey?"

Urban legend combined with a good dash of rumor suggests the Japanese gaming designer who finalized and packaged Donkey Kong didn't recognize the typo in the name. Originally slated to be "Monkey Kong," the game was shipped and the misspelling has long been absorbed in our social consciousness.

If any of you who have helped this book with content development and/or editing are expecting "Monkey Kong" and this looks more like "Donkey Kong," I take full responsibility for that.

I claim all the Donkey Kong–esque flaws that give this book character.

However, with its flaws I'm incredibly thankful for how this project turned out. My gratitude is for the community of discerning eyes and brilliant minds who helped bring this book to life. Your contributions were invaluable.

Like all big projects, this book involved a community's collaboration.

To Brent Graeve, Amey Victoria Adkins, and Rob O'Callaghan, I thank you for the tedious and laborious love you gave this project. If you were in my competitive reading group, you'd each be able to count this at least three times given how frequently and attentively you read the manuscript. Thanks.

I'd be remiss not to send some love and respect to Andrea Baker, Sarah Baldwin, Jason Byassee, David Chronic, Bethel Lee, Silvia Rodriguez, Silas West, Bo White, Tim Willard, and Jonathan Wilson-Hartgrove for taking a peek at bits of this along the way. Your suggestions and nudges towards clarity helped more than you know.

Just when I was about to give up, and when I thought I had run out of stories and illustrations, Jonathan Merritt showed up and pushed me over the edge. Thanks, brother, for all the hours shared in my little library; I still cherish those days together and all your encouragement and support.

David Hodges, thanks for your hospitality, especially when I needed to get out of my space and find an alternative writing lab. Your creativity and honestly lived life inspire me. So many of your songs are already on the soundtrack of my life, but specifically accompanied me during the writing of this book. I look forward to the many more that are being written inside you. Thank you for all the 3 AM conversations about community, friendship, and humanity.

To the guys at Dot&Cross, your spot became the last and most crucial creative zone this content was captured in. Corey Petrick, as an extrovert I thank you for providing silence, stillness, and space for me to be alone with these thoughts. Keep telling stories, we need more of them.

Of course, I want to communicate my gratitude and appreciation for Jessica Wong, Philis Boultinghouse, and all the good people at Howard Books for believing in the message and my ability to capture it. It's been great working with you.

Karen Ball, that was a lot of fun. Editing over Skype and passing the manuscript back and forth through Dropbox was surreal. Hope we can work together again soon.

Here goes a huge shout-out to my literary agent, Kathy Helmers. There are too many things to thank you for, but your advocacy and support has meant the world to me.

To each person whose stories and lives ended up in this book, and to the Word Made Flesh community—you've woven your stories into my own. I thank you for adding depth, texture, and enhancing our journeys to wholeness.

And last, but certainly not least, Phileena, thank you for teaching me everything I know about friendships, relationships, community, and, most important, love. I owe everything I've become to you and I look forward to stumbling through the rest of our lives together, learning to love and live and discover beauty in unlikely places.

Notes

PREFACE

SETTING THE TABLE:

COMMUNITY—WHY BOTHER?

1. The ethnic slur "Gypsy" has historically referred to Roma or Romani. The word "Gypsy" developed from the mistaken assumption that the Roma's heritage was Egyptian.

1

FAILURE:

THE PATCHES MAKE IT BEAUTIFUL

1. For one of the best articles on rethinking language, see Sarah Lance's blog post "Why I Don't Know Any Prostitutes . . ." at http://reclaimrestore.com/2012/02/19/why-i-dont-know -any-prostitutes/.

2. http://reclaimrestore.com/2012/05/18/names-2/.

3. Peter Rollins, *Fidelity of Betrayal: Towards a Church Beyond Belief* (Brewster, Mass.: Paraclete Press, 2008), 154–55.

2
DOUBT:
THE DIFFERENCE BETWEEN GOD AND SANTA

1. Paul Rase, "Questions I've Never Asked," *The Cry: The Advocacy Journal of Word Made Flesh* 9, no. 2 (Summer 2003): 16.

3
INSULATION:
FORGETTING THE FRAGRANCE

1. Henri J. M. Nouwen, *The Inner Voice of Love* (New York: Doubleday, 1996), 68.
2. Ibid.

6
THE UNKNOWN SELF:
THE SEARCH FOR SUTI SANA

1. Chris Sugden, *Seeking the Asian Face of Jesus: The Practice and Theology of Christian Social Witness in Indonesia and India 1974–1996* (Oxford: Regnum, 1997), 183–209.
2. Alexander Schmemann, *The Journals of Father Alexander Schmemann, 1973–1983* (Crestwood, NY: St. Vladimir's Seminary Press, 2002), 92.

7
BETRAYING COMMUNITY:
KISSING ONE ANOTHER TO DEATH

1. Donald Nicholl, *The Testing of Hearts: A Pilgrim's Journey,* ed. Adrian Hastings (London: Darton, Longman and Todd, 1998), 53.

2. Donald Nicholl, *The Testing of Hearts: A Pilgrim's Journey* (London: Lamp Press, London, 1989), 141–42.
3. Tuna's art and story are used with his consent. The lyrics of Matt Ammerman's song are also used with permission; see www.wordmadeflesh.org/updates/tuna/.

9

INGRATITUDE:

KILLING CHICKENS IN THE GOLDEN CITY

1. Kahlil Gibran, *The Prophet* (New York: Walker and Company, 1986), 37.
2. This story of the tucum ring was collaboratively developed by Esdrianne Cohen, Lília Marianno, Ben Miller, and Rich Nichols and is used in this text with their permission; it can also be found at www.wordmadeflesh.org/brazil/2009/03/story-of-the-tucum-ring/.

11

RESTLESSNESS:

FAITHFUL IN THE UNDRAMATIC

1. For a heartfelt and vulnerable memoir, check out Robert W. Ginn, *A Brilliant Career* (Xlibris, 2010).
2. "Where Are You Staying? (John 1:35–39a)," a baccalaureate sermon preached in Duke University Chapel on May 13–14, 2011, by the Reverend Dr. Sam Wells.
3. Ibid.

UNEXPECTED GIFTS

CHRISTOPHER L. HEUERTZ

Reading Group Guide

INTRODUCTION

From sitcoms to reality TV, the portrayal of our collective long-ing for connection and community is pervasive. The theme song of *Cheers* echoes in our ears: "Sometimes you want to go where everybody knows your name." And yet, if everyone wants com-munity, why is loneliness so common, even (sometimes espe-cially) within communities of faith? In his book, *Unexpected Gifts*, Chris Heuertz describes the counter-consumerism prac-tices and commitments that are necessary for communities of faith to grow and be sustained.

TOPICS AND QUESTIONS FOR DISCUSSION

1. What is the first thing that comes to your mind when you hear the word "community"? After reading this book, would you say you are living in community or are you

longing for community? Describe the contrast the author draws in the introduction between "connecting" together at The House of Loom and the necessary commitment of life together as a community.

2. The author describes eleven challenges that often show up in the midst of communities. Which one(s) did you identify with the most? Are there any you would add to the list?

3. How do you respond to failure—in your own life and in the lives of others? What qualities in a person or community does the author describe in chapter 1 that create the "safe space where a culture of confession is celebrated"? What are some specific ways you can cultivate these qualities in your life?

4. How are doubts about faith and God handled in your faith tradition? On page 24, the author quotes his priest's words: "the opposite of faith isn't doubt but certainty." Do you agree? Have you experienced a season of doubt in your life of faith? How did you respond to your doubts? Describe ways that worshipping together can be a sustaining practice in response to doubt within a community.

5. The author quotes Dietrich Bonhoeffer at the beginning of chapter 3: "Let [those] who cannot be alone beware of community . . . Let [those] who [are] not in community beware of being alone." With which group do you most identify (i.e., cannot be alone or not in community)? What are some gifts of solitude? Have you experienced solitude and/or sabbatical as an enriching gift to your life in community? Describe.

6. On page 51, the author proposes reviewing the last ten calls or texts made on your cell phone to highlight the diversity of your relationships. What did you learn about your relationships as a result of this exercise? What are some common attitudes and practices you have observed that create a spirit of openness and inclusion within a community?

7. On pages 84 to 87, the author describes phases that often follow a transition within a community. Can you relate these phases to a time when you decided to leave a group, church, community, etc.? How did you respond to these phases (even though you may not have named them at the time)? Throughout chapter 5, the author mentions several factors that, when present, contribute to transitions that are honoring and affirming for everyone involved. Make a list of these factors and discuss ways that they can be encouraged and nurtured.

8. Are there any transitions you have been part of that ended with hurt and unresolved conflict? In chapter 5, the author describes the process of communication he initiated in an effort to restore and reconcile hurtful transitions from Word Made Flesh. Are there any principles from this story that you sense God leading you to apply in unresolved conflicts in your life?

9. On page 97, the author lists three lies that lead to flawed identity: "I am what I have," "I am what I do," and "I am what other people think about me." Which of these is the greatest temptation for you? What are the most common

names you call yourself (other than your given name)? When you hear the name "Beloved," what is your response?

10. In chapter 6, the author highlights various scriptures that point to the restoration of humanity in Christ. How do you feel about your human needs, desires, and limitations? How do the author's reflections about embracing your humanity in chapter 6 impact you? St. Irenaeus is quoted as saying, "The glory of God is a human being fully alive." In light of this chapter's reflections, what might this phrase mean?

11. What is your response to the author's beginning assumption in chapter 7: "However it happens, all of us betray our communities and friendships and all of us are betrayed by them"? Have you experienced betrayal in a relationship? How did you respond? Have you experienced someone's "fidelity to love in the midst of betrayal"?

12. How did the story of the author's friendship with Tuna (page 120) impact you? Do you relate to the author's reflection that "most of our friendships can be incredibly self-serving or self-affirming"? Do you have friends in your life who have loved you, regardless of your accomplishments or failures? What is required to be that kind of friend?

13. How have communities you have been part of modeled relationships between men and women? What does the author propose as an alternative to avoidance in approaching the inevitability of attraction and chemistry within a community? What is your response to the author's recommendations?

14. On page 151, the author says: "A good host needs a good guest." What are qualities of a good host, based on your experiences? What are qualities of a good guest?

15. When you receive a gift (or compliment), how do you respond? What is the difference between acknowledging a gift and gratitude?

16. In chapter 10, the author relays the graphic story of the reign of the Khmer Rouge in Cambodia. How did reading this story impact you? What is your response to injustice and suffering in the world?

17. The author describes the decision he and his wife made to remain childless, choosing to live their lives on behalf of the "plundered childhood of many of our little friends, younger brothers and sisters." Are there choices you have made in your life to say "no" to something good so that you can say "yes" to something God is inviting you to give yourself to wholeheartedly? What spiritual practices are necessary to cultivate a heart that is available to listen and discern and then follow God's leading?

18. How are action and contemplative prayer related, according to the author's reflections at the end of Chapter 10? On page 173, the author defines centering prayer as "active consent to the divine presence of God." How is this similar to/different from the prayer you have practiced?

19. Has there been a time in your life when you chose to stay in a relationship or community when things got boring or didn't feel satisfying? What was the impact of staying—on

you and the relationship/community? In what ways do our cultural norms and practices encourage or discourage commitment and "staying"?

ENHANCE YOUR BOOK CLUB

1. After answering question #9 above, read "The Life of the Beloved" by Henri Nouwen. At your next book club, discuss the impact that embracing your belovedness (your true identity) has on the way you relate to others.

2. Commit to spend 20 minutes per day for one month practicing the contemplative prayer practice of *lectio divina* or centering prayer. Ask God for the grace to know and experience His love for you and to receive the name He calls you. Be still, listen, receive. Discuss your experiences at your next book club.

3. Pick one of the stories about injustice and suffering from *Unexpected Gifts* that particularly moved you. Spend some time asking God how you can be involved in fighting injustice and responding to suffering. Be aware of connections and opportunities that arise in response to your openness and availability. Discuss your experiences at your next book club.

4. Start a gratitude journal. Take 10 minutes at the end of each day to reflect on the day and enjoy and give thanks for the gifts you received through the day, both from God and from others. Or, write a letter to someone who has been a gift to your life, thanking them for their friendship and care. Discuss your experiences at your next book club.